PROBING THE
FRONTIERS

PROBING THE FRONTIERS

The Story of Pinkie Hill

John Lang

Roger and all me
With love

John

Jonathan Ball Publishers
Johannesburg

All rights reserved. No part of this publication may be reproduced or transmitted, in any form or by any means, without permission from the publishers.

© Rand Mines (Mining and Services) Ltd 1990

First published in 1990 by
Jonathan Ball Publishers
PO Box 2105
Parklands
2121

ISBN 0 947464 27 1

Typesetting and design by Book Productions, Pretoria
Printed and bound by National Book Printers, Goodwood, Cape

'The world belongs to the enthusiast who keeps cool.'

William McFee

Preface

The writing of this biography was an unforgettable experience for it brought me into association with Dr Francis George 'Pinkie' Hill, one of the greats of world mining, whose influence extended far wider than his distinguished contribution to mining technology.

He kindly spent many hours talking of days gone by, and made half-a-century's accumulation of personal and private files and papers freely available to me. Mrs Dora Hill, looking back across 54 years of marriage, gave invaluable guidance.

I am indebted to all those who so warmly responded to my request to share their memories of a valued colleague and friend. They included Mr P.H. Anderson, former Chairman, Rand Mines; Dr S. Biesheuvel, former Director, National Institute for Personnel Research, C.S.I.R.; Prof A.N. Brown, Head, Department of Mining Engineering, University of Pretoria; Prof H.G. Denkhaus, former Director, National Mechanical Engineering Institute, C.S.I.R.; Mr A.R.C. Fowler, former Consulting Engineer, Rand Mines; Mr T.L. Gibbs, former Government Mining Engineer; Mr R.T. Hofmeyr, former Director, Barlow Rand; the late Mr S.C. Newman, Chairman, Lonhro South Africa; Mr W.D. Ortlepp, Head, Rock Mechanics Department, Anglo American; Dr W.S. Rapson, former Research Adviser, Chamber of Mines of

South Africa; Mr G.V. Richdale, former President, Engelhard Industries Inc, Newark, New Jersey; Prof M.D.G. Salamon, Head, School of Mines, University of Colorado; Mr K.E. Steele, former General Manager, East Rand Proprietary Mines; Mrs Cynthia Tasker, Private Secretary to Mr Hill and, later, to Mr Newman; Mr. Edwin Thiel, former Consulting Engineer, Rand Mines; and the following associates at the University of the Witwatersrand: Prof R.W. Charlton, Principal and Vice-Chancellor; Prof G.R. Bozzoli, Principal and Vice-Chancellor, 1969–1977; Prof D.J. Du Plessis, Principal and Vice-Chancellor, 1978–83; Prof J.P.F. Sellschop, Deputy Vice-Chancellor (Research); and Prof R.P. Plewman, former Head, Department of Mining Engineering.

Finally, I am most grateful to Mr D.T. Watt, Chairman and Managing Director, Rand Mines, for suggesting this assignment, and to Mr Marshall Murton, Administration Manager, for his assistance and friendly encouragement.

John Lang

Contents

Chapter One:	A Miner at Oxford	1
Chapter Two:	'You must be mad to choose mining, Hill'	19
Chapter Three:	It's a Battlefield	33
Chapter Four:	The Road Away From Hell	43
Chapter Five:	Manager, New Style	52
Chapter Six:	Harmony and Some Discord	66
Chapter Seven:	Alarms and Excursions	83
Chapter Eight:	Pushing Back the Boundaries	102
Chapter Nine:	Some You Win	121
Chapter Ten:	The Academic Streak	139
Chapter Eleven:	Salt of the Earth	161

CHAPTER ONE

A Miner at Oxford

'Now Hill, don't become immersed in materialism'.

Whether the parting injunction was necessary or not, the words stuck in Hill's mind, for they rounded off an unforgettable year at Oxford reading English literature under C.S. Lewis, one of the truly creative literary minds of the day.

Young Francis George 'Pinkie' Hill, the first mining graduate to be elected a Rhodes scholar, was destined to become one of the greats of world mining, the doyen of those who would lead a quiet revolution in South Africa's deep-mining technology, and inspire a new enlightenment in employee relations on the mines.

On acceptance at New College, Oxford, he had chosen to study law, and would benefit profoundly in the years to follow from an enhanced lucidity of mind in decision making. He worked hard at his law studies while making friends and enjoying university life to the full, and was capped B.A. Hons (Jurisprudence) in 1929 after two years instead of the customary three. Then he persuaded the Warden of New College to allow him to spend his final year at Oxford reading English literature free from the restraints of exam taking.

Lewis, Fellow of Magdalen, suggested works for him to study, including those of Shakespeare, Milton and Matthew Arnold, and encouraged him to write essays, not

1

on their general content, but on the questions they raised for him personally, and on those propositions which seemed to him debatable. Though Hill remained unaware of it, Lewis in the Trinity Term of 1929 had undergone the conversion from atheism to Christianity which he was to describe much later in *Surprised By Joy*, and which was to shape his life as a Christian writer without peer in modern times.

Lewis was destined for fame as the author of about 40 books ranging from *The Screwtape Letters* to *The Chronicles of Narnia*. Today there are more books in print about Lewis than by him. Reviewing the latest biography, Brian Sibley wrote in *The Spectator* on 17 February, 1990: 'The man who discovered Narnia and the demonic correspondence of Screwtape seems destined for that immortality accorded to those with a genius for originality'. When Hill studied under the 31-year-old 'Jack' Lewis he was already renowned as a tutor. Hill never forgot the unique atmosphere of those quiet talks.

Whether it was Lewis in particular, or the ancient colleges of learning in general, it is indisputable that the experience of Oxford left its mark on Hill, emphasizing in him the determination to seek new and better ways of exercising his chosen profession of mining, and always, to give special consideration to the human factors involved.

On entering the University of the Witwatersrand in 1924, Hill had become known to J.H. Hofmeyr who, at the age of 27, had been appointed the University's first principal. Before leaving for Oxford, Hill was invited to spend a few days at Pretoria with Hofmeyr, the then Administrator of the Transvaal and on the threshold of an illustrious career in political life. There were long talks in which Hofmeyr stressed all that Oxford had to contribute to broadening a man's approach to life. Thereafter Hofmeyr kept in touch and visited Hill at Oxford. When the Oxford phase of Hill's life came to an end he wrote to Hofmeyr to tell him of a decision portending, for a mining man in those days, a novel change of direction. He planned to spend the year of a postgraduate scholarship awarded him by the Chamber of Mines in studying in Europe and the United States a subject then largely discounted in South Africa — industrial psychology, covering the spectrum of employee relations and personnel management.

Hofmeyr replied:

> You seem to have made the most of Oxford – I am more than glad. I can see that Oxford had meant much to you – it always does to anyone who goes there with the eyes to see and the readiness to receive impressions. The man who is self-assured and 'cocky' and set in his opinions rarely gets from it what he should. I seem to remember giving you fatherly advice when you were elected a Rhodes Scholar, to the effect that you should try to be less retiring and more self-assured. This year, I have been giving the Rhodes Scholar whom we have just elected exactly the opposite advice! There is a golden mean in all things.

Of Hill's decision to study industrial psychology, Hofmeyr commented:

> You seem to have struck out on an interesting line of investigation, and we shall all be the better for its application in South African conditions. But, as you have come to see so clearly, we do struggle with a most burdensome handicap in the form of our prejudices in the matter of colour. Somehow we have got to be brought to regard the native as a co-worker, and not merely as a chattel and a serf, but old prejudices die hard, and you

dare not ride rough-shod over them. Yet I see a great deal of hope in the changing attitude of our university students. There is undoubtedly a considerable increase of real thinking in our universities and for the most part it is on liberal lines. I hope it will grow sufficiently in volume and will assert itself soon enough to save South Africa.

Alas for poor Hofmeyr and those who shared his open mind! A substantial shift in white attitudes towards the advancement of Black South Africans lay far in the future beyond his life-span. He would be a man on a rack, torn between his vision of South Africa's fate, and the obligation, as he saw it, to modify his policies in the interests of meaningful leadership in contemporary political life. Hill would be bound in turn by the statutory conditions that governed his working life, and would find his fulfillment in a drive to create a safer, healthier and more congenial mining environment for men to work in.

Hill was born in Kroonstad, Orange Free State, on 29 April, 1905, the second son of the town's attorney, also named Francis George. His mother, Katherine Johanna, born Hauptfleisch, was the descendant of Dutch settlers at Wellington in the Cape. Hill's grandfather, Samuel George, was a builder in Natal who was attracted to Kimberley soon after the discovery of the diamond fields. He found the roaring life-style of the diggers too ungodly and set off to trek back to Natal. He paused at Kroonstad, the settlement on the banks of the Valsch River which the railway had just reached from Natal, and he perceived the opportunities for a man of his craft in the growing township. Hill's father, Francis George senior, had qualified as an attorney there when war broke out in 1899. A loyal Free Stater, he rode with the Kroonstad Commando to invade Natal and lay siege to Ladysmith; later he became chief commissariat officer to the Boer forces at Smaldeel (now Theunissen). After the war he returned to Kroonstad to practise as an attorney on his own account. He became town councillor, was mayor several times, and served as a circuit steward of the Wesleyan Church.

In these capacities Hill's father served the community in a diversity of religious, educational and cultural endeavours. He was *bloedsap*, staunchly supporting General Smuts' South African Party, and stood for the Provincial Council in a forlorn hope bid in 1923. He married young, and built the lovely Hill home 'The Terraces' on the banks of the river; and there raised four sons (a fifth died in infancy), and two daughters. The children grew up in what were, in some ways, idyllic conditions. There was a clear sense of Christian purpose, but there was a great deal of fun too with tennis parties, swimming and boating on the river, croquet on the lawn and golf on the town links. There were afternoon teas on the lawn and garden parties, and seaside holidays at the Cape with visits to cousins in the winelands. 'The days of our carefree youth' declares a caption stencilled by young Francis under a 1913 snapshot in his personal album showing the family perched on Muizenberg mountain.

As Francis grew into his 'teens he was captivated by visions of the Royal Navy. His father owned a copy of *Jane's Fighting Ships* and Hill followed the adventures of British warships through the 1914-18 War, sorrowful when the unhappy fortunes of war called for them to be struck from the list. He set his heart on a naval career and persuaded his father to enter him at the Royal Navy Academy at Dartmouth, only to suffer heart-break at the news that he was three months past the maximum entry age of 13 years 9 months. He went off instead to Kingswood College at Grahamstown where he was much influenced by an outstanding History and English master, H.T. Crouch, later to be headmaster of Dale College, King Williams Town. Crouch, Hill recalls, had a remarkable talent to arouse in schoolboys both the sporting instinct and a perception of the satisfying joys of scholarship. In later life he wrote to Hill:

> If I had the pennies I would go abroad very regularly since so much of the glory of the world is tucked away in the corners of Europe, particularly in one small island.

One can be sure that Hill was properly prepared by Crouch and Hofmeyr for Oxford which Matthew Arnold described as 'that sweet city of dreaming spires' and, less familiarly, as 'whispering from her towers the last enchantments of the Middle Age ...'. Surely a long haul from the galleries of Robinson Deep, 8 000 feet below surface, which Hill encountered as a mining student in South Africa.

Hill had been attracted in some degree to his father's profession of law, but came to realise that the family business was the natural heritage of his elder brother, Sonnie. Then from a young neighbour who came courting one of his sisters he was given a romantic picture of mining through colourful tales of the small gold mines in the lovely hills and valleys of Pilgrim's Rest in the Eastern Transvaal.

> I gained the impression that one rode out into the wide open spaces on horseback to prospect for minerals. With this picture in mind I decided to make mining my career.

There were then no gold mines in the Orange Free State to contrast the stark realities of deep mining with the fantasies of an open air life amid scenes of natural beauty. Hill became one of a handful of South Africans studying for a degree in mining engineering, and in 1924 entered the University of the Witwatersrand created two years previously out of the old School of Mines. He was by then a strikingly good-looking young man, with the wiry, athletic build of a scrum half. His height, like that of his three brothers, was below the average for a South African, and earned him some joshing at school and the nickname 'Pinkie' which would stay for a lifetime.

Hill denies any outstanding aptitude for sport, but he played for first teams both at Kingswood College and at University, representing Wits at rugby (as scrum half), hockey and tennis, and was captain of cricket there. What he may have lacked in brilliance he made up in determination. As a new junior at Kingswood College he had his first experience of cross-country running, for which he had no physiological capacity whatsoever, and stayed up with the leaders of the senior boys until he fell unconscious. Back home at Kroonstad, for a dare, he swam the five miles of the Valsch between dam wall and rapids. He would retain his athleticism throughout life, despite the early onset of gout and arthritis, and found his particular satisfaction in golf, holding his handicap under 10 for 50 years, and taking a team of senior golfers to tour Britain in his seventies.

A brilliant sportsman he may not have been, but he was good enough to enjoy sport to the full and the companionship that went with it. His sporting and academic achievements at Wits, and his involvement in student affairs, were easily strong enough to qualify him as the all-rounder required by the rules of the Rhodes Scholarship.

His brothers and sisters proved good university material as well. The elder sister Katherine (Renie) went to London to qualify as a doctor, one of the first South African women to do so. Her sister Winnie became a teacher of music. Sonnie, after graduating at the University of Cape Town became a partner in his father's legal business. David and Denston also went to UCT to study accountancy. There David, another scrum half (as all four brothers were), would delight his sport-loving father by selection to play against the touring All-Blacks for both the University and the Combined Cape Town Clubs. Newspaper cuttings of the University's narrow defeat, and the Combined Clubs' narrow victory, survive in the family records.

At Wits, Pinkie Hill found not only work and sport, and male companionship. There were also girls, and he enjoyed their company, cultivating an eye and an empathy for a good-looking lass that would never desert him. The photo album holds a good selection of young ladies, and among casual friends of the time were the two daughters of Sir Robert Kotzé, the distinguished Government Mining Engineer. To one of them, Dora, he would return some years later as a serious suitor.

In the meantime, there were dances, about once a week, which Hill rarely missed. But young men were relatively innocent in those days, especially those from country places.

> We grew up in a very straight-laced fashion at Kroonstad. And at University sleeping around was unheard of. We all had girl friends but I don't know anyone who actually slept with girls at Wits. We used to play tennis with them and go to dances.

With Pinkie at Oxford; Renie with her husband in Tanganyika (though she came home to 'The Terraces' for the birth of her first child, yet another Francis); with David at the University of Cape Town, and Denston, the youngest at Kingswood College, Grahamstown, their father dictated fortnightly a joint letter, headed 'My Dear Children' and concluding 'Your Affectionate Daddy'. His letter of 4 January, 1928 opens:

> As you may know I generally have each year's letters bound, so that in the years to come they should prove interesting ... .

They do indeed.

The bound volume surviving entitled 'Letters from Home', and covering the years 1928–1929, contains the following, dated 22 May, 1928.

> In Francis' letter to hand this morning he mentions he had had a visit from Professor Hofmeyr. One wonders what will be the future of Hofmeyr who will be returning to South Africa two days before the General Election takes place ... he appears to have definitely thrown in his lot with the South African Party, and there are those who look upon him as the future leader of the party after General Smuts retires.

Meanwhile Francis, busy with the finer points of jurisprudence, had sought relaxation and diversity of interest in the University Air Squadron.

> I enjoyed that. For one thing one was enabled to learn how to fly, and to fly well. I joined the Royal Air Force Reserve, got my wings, and became a Flight Lieutenant. The other thing I valued was the bigger range of friendship, the wider circle.

The 'Letter from Home' of 15 August says:

> This morning's English mail brings a long letter from

Francis giving us a description of his life at the Aerodrome. They do a little flying during the day, but the rest of the time is spent just as they like as long as they do not leave the vicinity of the aerodrome. He has had two solo flights, and during one of them looped the loop which seems to be rather a risky thing to do the second time that one goes up.

In September came another long letter from Francis redolent with a young man's joy in the first experience of solo flight. He reports that he has completed flying training without as much as damaging an aeroplane, and nonchalantly reveals what he has previously concealed, that flying training in those days was extremely hazardous.

> About seven of our planes have come to grief while I have been here — but in only one case was the accident fatal. The accidents were in nearly all cases due to bad landings or forced landings — and in fact are so seldom fatal that they are looked upon as a joke rather than otherwise... .
>
> For finishing dual I had to do my five hours solo, during the course of which I had to do two tests — a height test and a cross-country flight to any other aerodrome at least 50 miles off. The day on which I did my flight test proved to be very cloudy.. . These proved to be a good way up, but at 10 000 feet I came above them — and it was well worth the climb (which took about 20 minutes). Words fail to give an adequate description ... I flitted about in this little world of my own for about 10 minutes, switched off and commenced gliding down. From 10 000 feet one can glide for about 16 miles, and I had little difficulty in reaching the aerodrome without the engine ... this being the test, to fly down from 10 000 feet without the engine — and land the plane.

The airfield Hill chose for the cross-country solo flight the next day was Manston near the Kent coast, to become renowned in 1940 as one of the hot spots of the Battle of Britain. The letter contains a sketch of the route taken from Stag Lane north of London, crossing the Thames and following a course south of its Estuary to RAF Manston, then returning by a southerly route skirting Canterbury. He wrote:

> As I approached the Thames it became very misty and to see the ground at all well, one had to stay at about 1 000 feet. One has a map by which to fly and I had little difficulty in picking up landmarks — from the air one gets a very clear view of the meandering nature of the Thames — it was quite alive with craft of various sorts moving slowly through water as muddy as that of the Valsch River at its worst. I think I managed to pass *between* the two prohibited areas — prohibited I believe because of gun firing practice ... I landed safely, the 70 miles taking me about 42 minutes, thanks to a following wind — and after receiving a certificate from the officer of the watch to the effect that I had arrived and made a good landing, I took off once more.

Hill then recounts that he decided to see a bit of Kent before returning, so set off to Penshurst where he had spent a week as a guest of a Mrs Wood.

He had little difficulty in finding the house and circled above it at about 400 feet but failed to attract the attention of any of those living there. He next took a look at the Crystal Palace, then climbed and was soon skimming the tops of clouds at 5 000 feet trying (vainly it proved) to get photographs to record the splendour of the swirling cloud mass.

Before long Stag Lane appeared and my 40 hours were completed. But it had been great from more points of view than one. In the first place, there was a good crowd of fellows there — nearly all undergrads, either from Oxford or Cambridge, and we got on very well. Also — during the course of the last few weeks I met a couple of girls employed at De Havillands' (in the drawing office) — a chance event leading to a tennis party one Saturday afternoon — and a couple of dances, which were most enjoyable. Then of course I have learned to fly — not only for nothing — I was paid to do so.

Hill goes on to discuss his plans, after the five weeks with the air squadron, of getting down to serious work in a small cottage on the Cornish coast with a cove for swimming when the tide was out — an ideal situation suggested by Lady Knox, whose husband General Knox had taken part in the occupation of the Orange Free State by British forces in 1900, and commandeered 'The Terraces' as his headquarters.

Most of the 'Letters from Home' deal with the parochial events of small town life, with meetings of Kroonstad Council, and of bodies like the Graves Committee caring for three cemeteries, two military and one for those who died in Kitchener's concentration camps of 1900–1902. They tell of weddings, church fêtes, synods and harvest festivals, of school plays, of the comings and goings of family and friends, and of joy and sorrow.

A year after Hill penned his zestful account of the experience of flight, his father wrote of a tragic event already notified by telegram, that his brother David, riding a newly-bought motor cycle, had skidded on a Cape Town tramline, and died from head injuries.

Suddenly without a moment's warning he has been taken from us ... we have been left to mourn the loss of the loved one. And so we leave him in God's hand, knowing He cannot make a mistake.

The news took time to reach Hill who had travelled across Europe and was representing South African students at an international conference in Budapest. Realising the impact of the tragedy on his mother and father, Hill would thereafter reach a painful resolution — he gave up the flying he loved to lessen their fears of further bereavement.

From Budapest he drove to Greece with two companions. One was Herbert Hart, a man of learning and wit, who was to become Professor of Jurisprudence at Oxford and a jurist of international repute. The other member of the troika was an Australian, learned in classics, later to become an eminent member of the Australian Parliament. It was a fantastic cultural experience, Hill recalls, to spend time in their company. They knew how to select the ancient sites to visit, and they too were filled with the exuberance of youth. One of the highlights was Olympia where the games in honour of Zeus were first celebrated in 776 BC, the festivals then including literature, art, drama, rhetoric, music and gymnastics. Hill recalls:

> At Olympia we thought we would emulate the Greek athletes. You know they often ran naked. The three of us undressed and ran around the stadium. There was nobody there — well, only one or two people.

Not long after that memorable tour, Hill left Oxford and embarked on his year-long study of industrial psychology. A natural starting point for his quest was Geneva, the centre of studies in the science of management and a driving force in its promotion. From Geneva, he moved to Britain and the United States.

His way through America was smoothed for him by friendships forged while at Oxford, and especially by Herbert Woodman, who became attorney with a big New York legal firm. Woodman settled down in a country home, an estate of 2 000 acres with a stream running through, which Hill would re-visit many times in the years ahead.

With doors opened everywhere, Hill drove 18 000 kilometres across the States in a second-hand Chevrolet bought for 75 dollars. He visited departmental stores, factories and mines, fuelling his enthusiasm for a specialized and humane approach to handling people at work. Characteristically, he made new friends and enjoyed himself in the company of young men and women. He remembers with particular pleasure the visit to the Copper Queen Mine on the borders of Mexico.

> I thought I would like to see something of American mining and the extent to which they were applying industrial psychology. It was obviously a delightful experience because I wasn't working for my living, I was just going underground and studying mining situations ... .
>
> I remember too we used to cross the border to dance in an hotel in a small Mexican town. Young men and girls from round about would come to dance and leave the old women who accompanied them outside. As you approached you would see the rows of chaperones seated outside in the street while the young folk enjoyed dancing on their own in the bar. Oh yes, and it was a bit of a trauma getting back across the border afterwards ... .

All his life Hill would leave a trail of raincoats, umbrellas and personal objects in his travelling wake, often returned by kindly friends from distant places. In Mexico it was not untypical for him to have left behind at the Copper Queen the passport required for his return through the US border post in the late night. A man of temperate habit, he enjoyed feigning dead-drunkenness at the border where the border guards good-naturedly allowed his friends to drive him through.

At the end of the American tour he found himself parking the Chevrolet outside the Cunard offices in New York. He had arranged to sell the car for 30 dollars.

> When I came out of the Cunard offices, all the handles had been wrenched off the locked doors in an attempt to get at my luggage. I had to rush off to find somebody who could open the car so that I could get my luggage to go on board the ship which was ready to raise the gangways. By the time I had rescued my luggage it was too late to dispose of the car as arranged. I parked it at the side of the ship and asked the porter who took my luggage what he would give for the Chevrolet. His answer was 'Five bucks'. He could see I was in a bit of a predicament. Anyway I sold him the car for five dollars. It was in beautiful condition with good tyres.

There had been much to enjoy in that marvellous year, but his enjoyment did not divert Hill's concentration from the gathering of observations and perceptions that would underline his approach to mining and the leadership of men for a lifetime. His thoroughness of approach comes through clearly in the notebook that survives recording his employment as a student miner at Scotland's Fife Coal Company in the winter of 1930/31. There were none of the pithead baths of today's collieries and young Pinkie went home to his lodgings, black with coal dust for his end-of-shift bath.

In South Africa the great strike and Rand Rebellion of 1922 were still fresh in memory. Even fresher in British minds was the General Strike of 1926. And now those bad times had given way to worse. The world was in the grip of the Great Depression signalled by the Wall Street Crash at the end of 1929. Industry and agriculture struggled to survive in a desert of deflation in which wage talks were about wage cuts, seldom or never about rises. Management was often harsh and authoritative, and as bad tempered as the angry unions. Retrenchment was the order of the day. Jobs were hard to come by and harder to hold; in both Britain and South Africa skilled and even professional men queued for a dole, or for labouring work at a few shillings a day. In the circumstances, the Fife colliery seems to have been fairly managed. It is nonetheless a pointer to Hill's unfoldment that his careful records of a diversity of technical matters of interest to the engineer, are balanced by an equal emphasis on the all important human factor.

> Several discussions today with regard to relations of men with managements. Apparently one reason for the success of the self-made agent or manager is that it is inborn in him to greet men and have one or two cheery words, that he still does so and they feel they are not being 'overlooked', that they are humans deserving some notice; the *manner* is everything — all aloofness, sullenness, or high-handedness should be avoided; all-important is the need for fairness (NB rates of pay) and keeping one's word. Before any drastic action is taken of sacking a man, every thought should be given to the case — avoid hastiness, as the repercussions of such an action

may be great; men start talking and the flames of grievances are easily fired by words.

Hill notes that modern methods tend to make the manager too much of a clerk, pushing papers, reports, records, around the managerial desk. He is losing personal contact with the men.

The human link is all-important in management — men must be made to feel that they are not merely cogs in a machine.

and again:

> Do not kill a man's initiative; let him have rope — scope for his own ideas; put forward suggestions and let these simmer, and if convinced of the rightness of these ideas keep on pressing them, and show some force — some drive, but always tactfully. *Do not become enmeshed in the detail of the work* — Give a man a chance — let him have opportunities of remedying errors and proving his abilities ... as far as possible instructions should be given in such a way as to make man below think that they are really his own ideas, perhaps slightly modified.

The importance of these observations, and others like them, is not that they were carefully written down and indexed in the 100 pages of a hard-covered graduate student's exercise book, for many such are filed and forgotten, but that Hill would apply them in principle and practice through four decades of a highly significant mining career. He had already become convinced of the importance of scientific management, and of the principles enunciated in the works of Frederick Winslow Taylor, and Taylor's works would become prescribed reading for Hill's subordinate managers in the years to come.

Hill's mind ranged over many other matters at the Fife Coal Company. He sees the need for a concentrated drive on safety, involving the men personally; he observes how the steady British miner is being pushed out of trade union councils by aggressive 'reds' of the radical left. He records that electric cap lamps have just been brought into use at Fife, and that the men now prefer them to the safety and acetylene lamps in former use; also that they are apparently uncomplaining about being charged three-halfpence a day for them out of the 10 to 12 shillings they earn.

He covers every aspect of the colliery operation, comments on what might usefully be employed in South Africa, and is critical of shortcomings in training, in communications, in systems. Then in a final paragraph he writes:

> Dr Miles tells me of Mr Stevenson's activities in South Africa — for two years he has been at the New Modder, where Mr Meyer is manager. Mr Meyer, he says, is great on (Frederick Winslow) Taylor — many cheers!

On his return to South Africa Hill went to see E.C.J. Meyer, member of a notable mining family, and was signed on at New Modder, the gold mine on the East Rand administered by Rand Mines, since pioneer days the dominant mining house on the Rand.

CHAPTER TWO

'You must be mad to choose mining, Hill'

Back in 1924 when Hill was an 18-year-old student at Wits he had been sent to the old Robinson Deep for practical training during his vacation. There for the first time he faced the harsh realities of gold mining on the Rand.

> It was the shock of my life! I thought, 'My God what have I let myself in for? Instead of being out in the open air, here am I crawling around in the bowels of the earth'.

The rank-and-file miners didn't help. It was beyond their comprehension that somebody with Hill's potential should opt for mining. He worked under a hard-bitten sampler who urged him:

> Go to the Springkell Sanatorium and see the miners coughing up their lungs from phthisis. If you stay in this game, like them, your life will be a short one. A man of your abilities must be mad to choose mining.

Hill recalls black periods of doubt when he sat on a mine dump really 'down in the dumps' at the choice he had made. Mining companies did not encourage nor care for young entrants as they do today. Accommodation was rough and ready — a mattress on the floor of the single quarters in a mine dating back to the nineteenth century. One of the jobs given him was the inspection far underground of launders used to duct a mixture of sand and water from the sand dumps on surface to provide a sand-filling for worked-out areas of the mine. On one occasion, accompanied by a single Black worker, he was in a remote and deserted tunnel checking that the flow in the launders was unimpeded. The Black miner went off leaving young Hill alone. He sat down to wait. At that moment his carbide lamp failed.

He sat alone in the absence of light known only to miners, took out his lunch sandwiches, opened the package and laid them beside him. He paused for a while with his thoughts in that absolute blackness; then reached out for a sandwich — and put his hand on a rat busy devouring it. At that moment he asked himself whether he was not after all mad to go mining, and during further vacation courses on mines he spent sleepless hours, wondering. However —

> I decided to stay with it — and I never regretted the decision. It has been a life full of challenge — always some problem to face and overcome... a fascinating life.

Others lacked his staying power. Mining was unpopular in those days because of the unpleasant and hazardous environment underground, and the fear of miners' phthisis or silicosis, the disease of the lungs caused by breathing concentrations of dust permeated by microscopic particles of abrasive quartz. There were few entrants into the Department of Mining Engineering at Wits. Only about three students were graduating yearly when Hill entered in 1924, and the industry was dependent on an intake from British and other mining schools.

After the first year Hill won the Hennen Jennings Scholarship for the best pupil and went on to win the Chamber of Mines Scholarship and Gold Medal on graduation. Hill wryly dismisses these achievements as unexceptional because of the paucity of competition. He was proud however of the Rhodes Scholarship, and the combined benefits of his three scholarships enabled him to continue as a student until he began work as a highly-qualified 27-year-old. He then had to prove himself as a leader of men. Mining was a tough life calling for the ability to inspire men to work under you in rugged circumstances. An impressive list of academic achievements was not enough, and many a graduate so armed has proved a failure under the stress of practical mining.

Hill soon proved himself, but not without a brief stumble as he faced up to the practical expertise called for in acquiring the necessary certificate of competency in mine management. Edwin W. Thiel, a career-long colleague and friend, recalls:

> In 1934, we sat together at New Modder mine for our mine manager's ticket. I passed, and Pinkie failed. He was a little short of practical experience. However, he soon sat again and passed.

Hill had joined the New Modder on 4 January, 1932. It was a big mine for those days, milling between 150 000 and 250 000 tons of gold-bearing ore a month. It was fortunate to have in E.C.J. Meyer, an able and methodical manager, ahead of his time, who had set up the most advanced planning department in the industry. He appointed Hill to the department as his personal assistant. Meyer would start his rounds of the mine at 6 a.m., a highly unusual time for a manager to be up and around. Hill would accompany him to the shaftheads where underground managers would report on the previous days' production, accidents, labour incidents and so on, and Hill would record the discussions.

Regularly, Meyer would hold meetings at which papers were read on scientific management, industrial psychology and so on. Hill persuaded him to introduce some system into the hiring and firing of employees by setting up an employment office under Hill's control, the forerunner of major developments to come.

Meyer was the son of a missionary who had given his children a university education. Hill remembers them as a cultured, hard-working and delightful family. He was fortunate too in that he met other congenial families at the mine, and enjoyed their company and the opportunities for sport.

Not everybody entering mining those days was so lucky. Bluff, burly A.R.C. 'Buster' Fowler, who was to be a lifelong friend, chose mining engineering after matriculation in 1929 because the Depression had hit South Africa and he could see no work for a graduate outside mining. He was one of many who would enter mining at the time for the same reason and rise to high positions in the industry. Though he enjoyed the rough and tumble of mine life when he signed on at a mine after graduation, he found the management harsh and overbearing.

> Jobs were so hard to get that you found men with managerial qualifications doing run-of-the-mill mining work, and trained surveyors chipping rock for sampling. Married men were glad to have any kind of job at all. I was not in that position so that I could take life philosophically. I was underground one day and the bloody underground manager comes along — he used to wear braces — and a whole entourage of brass behind him. He starts blowing me up for no good reason. Just throwing his weight around. After the shift I went to his office and demanded to talk to him about what happened

underground. He gets out from behind his desk and comes at me shouting, 'This isn't a kindergarden.' I said, 'Look, touch me and you're out of that window.' I was fit and strong you see — I would've torn him apart. He calmed down at once and said: 'Quite right, my boy' — and asked me to dinner at his house two days later. But you had to be tough — to be prepared to throw your job in. Others couldn't do it because they had wives and families, and no hope of another job.

Hill adapted quickly to the mining environment. At New Modder some of the stopes where the gold-bearing ore was broken out, were very low.

You couldn't sit upright; they had what were called arse pads, you tied them round and you sat on your bottom and slid down the stopes which were inclined about 25 degrees. The narrowness of the stopes didn't matter to me — when you are young you take these things in your stride. I remember one chap though, a shift boss on New Modder called Fraser. He was over 6-foot, and he said to me one day, 'My God, you know, I can't take this mining, sliding down these bloody stopes!' So he gave it up, and started a transport company which became a huge thing.

Hill received rapid promotion, becoming Chief in the Planning Department in November 1933, and Section Manager in July 1935. Soon after this came an essential milestone. He had resumed his friendship with Dora Kotzé whom he had met at Wits and again while at Oxford. Dora took a degree in Geography at Newnham College, Cambridge. She visited Oxford as captain of the Cambridge women's tennis team: and Hill was called upon to umpire the match. Thereafter they went their separate ways, but back in South Africa time and circumstance brought them together again. This time they fell in love and were married on 7 March, 1936.

Ahead lay a life-long love-match, deeply affectionate, mutually supportive in their distinctive ways, staunchly so in Hill's, fiercely so in Dora's. Dora was a forthright and lively companion through Hill's increasingly busy and sometimes controversial life, providing a strong home base and bearing him two sons and two daughters. The Hills would become known to a widening circle as kindly companions with a zest both for work and leisure, always great fun to be with.

With marriage came a close association between Hill and his father-in-law, Sir Robert Kotzé, a man who profoundly influenced the growth of South African mining. He was born in Darling, Cape, in 1870, the son of a Dutch Reformed Church minister with liberal views who, in his early career, endured trial for heresy. Robert's uncle was Sir John Kotzé, Chief Justice of the Transvaal Republic, until dismissed by President Paul Kruger for seeking to exercise a testing right over decisions of the Volksraad.

Young Robert grew up as a country boy in the Cape, but showed intellectual brilliance and attended the Royal School of Mines in Britain and the Academy of Mining at Clausthal in Germany. He became Government Mining Engineer of the Transvaal when the colony was granted self-government in 1908. He was the architect of the Precious and Base Metals Act of 1908 to be commonly known, like its predecessor, as The Gold Law. Though substantially amended over time, it would continue in force for nearly 60 years. He was a pioneer in promoting mine safety and the combating of silicosis, the miner's scourge in the earlier days of mining. Dora Hill comments: 'I was lucky in having two great humanitarians in my life. My father and my husband.'

Robert Kotzé was a strong believer in the principle that mineral wealth belonged essentially to the State. He vested in the Gold Law the right of the Crown to mine for precious metals and to dispose of them, introducing the system whereby the State could lease to any person the exclusive right to mine gold in a proclaimed area. Thus, instead of proclaiming areas open for public pegging, the Government called for tenders for mining under lease.

Since then the State has been a sleeping partner in most gold mining operations, recognising that mining on the Rand was a massive operation involving the complex aggregation of funds by private enterprise. In this way the Treasury was assured of a share, much more than fair some say, of the profits, while the potential return to shareholders was attractive enough to ensure the essential capital investment. Kotzé's design of the lease scheme brought him a knighthood at a relatively early age.

On the union of the former colonies in 1910 Sir Robert became the first Government Mining Engineer of South Africa; he built up the Mines Department as a prestigious arm of South African mining, deploying great expertise. He was a leading crusader for mine safety, working closely with the Chamber of Mines, and addressed vigorously the problem of silicosis, personally inventing the konimeter, of international importance as the first effective instrument for measuring the concentration of harmful dust in mine air. He became an influential figure close to the Cabinet, and a confidant of Smuts.

When Hertzog succeeded Smuts in 1927 however Kotzé, no man's lackey, soon clashed with the Government over the appointment of a political nominee as Chief Inspector of Machinery, and resigned his office, only shortly after becoming the first South African to receive the Gold Medal of the Institute for Mining and Metallurgy in London. Smuts described the affair as a 'gross and outrageous injustice'. Kotzé continued his association with mining as a mining house consultant and director.

His zeal and energy in promoting the ideals of safety and health would have their spin-off in Hill's own career; and in 1954 he would acknowledge Sir Robert's contribution to mining by making it the subject of his presidential address to the Associated Scientific and Technical Societies.

Hill himself came to know Smuts while at New Modder. Smuts' son Japie took up mining as a career and he and Hill became friendly, resulting in frequent invitations to spend weekends at the Smuts' home at Irene in the countryside near Pretoria. Hill found the simplicity of the Smuts' lifestyle remarkable. It was perhaps fortunate for Hill that his early fantasy of mining as a life spent prospecting on horseback did not materialise. At Irene he found he was no horseman, and the Smuts' family custom of Sunday morning gallops across the veld proved for him an excruciating experience.

However, for his friend, Buster Fowler, the dream was clothed with some reality. Head Office became aware that he was growing restive on the East Rand. Fortunately, someone was intelligent enough to preserve his great promise for Rand Mines by transferring him to Pilgrim's Rest. There the group managed, as a single operation, a number of small mines scattered in the remote and lovely hills surrounding the village. Fowler recalls:

> I really loved it up there. I thought: it's worthwhile even if they don't pay me! When I first went to Pilgrim's Rest, I asked: 'How do I go to work?' The reply was: 'There are five horses in the stable. You must take the right horse

though; the one horse goes to Theta mine and the other to Brown's Hill. If you get on the Brown's Hill horse there's no way you'll ever get to Theta'.

Hill remembers that Smuts tended to be uncommunicative, buried in his own deep thoughts. The association however led him to study with appreciation Smuts' essay into philosophy: 'Holism and Evolution' with its emphasis on the essential interdependence of all creation. Hill did not retain the Wesleyan faith of his father and mother, but finding himself, like Smuts, at variance with certain of the theological concepts of his upbringing, he evolved a personal philosophy of life. Hill came to take a deep interest in the origins and evolution of the universe, and the meaning of life. While accepting that there was much that could not be comprehended he saw against the background of his reading in science and the humanities, a controlling and guiding force in the universe and human affairs.

In June, 1937, Hill was seconded to Rand Mines in Johannesburg for two years as assistant to the Consulting Engineer, A.J. Walton. Rand Mines was the Johannesburg arm of Central Mining and Investment Corporation, London, the successor to the Wernher, Beit and Hermann Eckstein partnerships founded in the pioneer days of South African diamond and gold mining. Rand Mines administered the South African interests of the group, but new departures and ventures, and important decisions, required the approval of the Board of Central Mining, which also appointed the consulting engineers in Johannesburg.

Walton, under whom Hill now worked, was a notable personality. He had joined the group in 1910. As part of a drive to reorganise the group on a more cost-efficient basis, it had been decided to appoint managers from the British collieries, noted for scrutinising costs down to the last sixpence. Walton, the young manager of the Bogillt colliery in North Wales, was one of those appointed. He became manager of the Rose Deep, and then General Manager of Crown Mines from 1919–1936, establishing it as one of the great mines of the world. He lived to 95, a wise old man steeped in the lore of the Rand.

His associate R.S.G. Stokes, another of the great aristocracy of consulting engineers, would live one year longer than Walton. After service in the South African War as a trooper, followed by a short spell on Crown Mines, Ralph Stokes became mining editor of the *Rand Daily Mail*, leading to a two-year tour around the world and the publication of his book *Mines and Minerals of the British Empire*. After a varied mining career he became a consulting engineer of Rand Mines in 1928, and subsequently a Head Office manager. He believed strongly in a scientific approach to the solution of problems at a time when mining engineers generally preferred to rely on accumulated experience. He had served as an officer in the Royal Engineers in the First World War with distinction, and would do so again in the Second. He was awarded the DSO and the MC for gallantry and ended his military career as a brigadier and Commander of the Bath. After his death in 1979 the SA Institute of Mining and Metallugy created the Brigadier Stokes Memorial Award, regarded as the premier accolade for achievement in the mining industry.

When Hill reported for duty with these two outstanding men in Johannesburg, the mining industry was at the peak of the expansion sparked by the departure of major trading countries from the Gold Standard in the wake of the Great Depression. By the end of 1935, the gold price, pegged for 200 years at the standard price of four pounds five shillings an ounce, had jumped 45 per cent. The prospects of the gold mines were transformed. Huge blocks of gold-bearing ore previously said to be not worth a penny of capital expenditure became payable, not just in existing fields, but in the new gold-fields that now beckoned the entrepreneur. By 1936, fifteen new mines were being opened up and 23 main vertical shafts were being sunk on them, while another 13 were going down on existing mines.

The new mines were mostly on the East Rand, but one, Venterspost, was being sunk by Gold Fields on a wholly new field, the Far West Rand — the first of 15 which would include the most profitable of all time. In 1930, while South Africa was still in the grip of the Depression, Gold Fields, facing a bleak future as its mines began to peter out, had launched a search for the continuation of the Main Reef westwards towards Potchefstroom and the Mooi River. The search was sparked by Dr Rudolph Krahmann, a pioneer of geophysical prospecting, employing a magnetometer to trace the course of the 'missing' reefs. Krahmann claimed that by using the magnetometer he would be able to read the course of the magnetic shales found elsewhere in association with the gold-bearing reef, and he was backed by Gold Fields' brilliant consulting engineer, Guy Carleton Jones.

To finance the exploration Gold Fields formed the West Witwatersrand Areas Ltd, and offered a major participation to Rand Mines. John Martin, then chairman of Rand Mines, recommended a conditional acceptance, but the Board of Central Mining in distant London, which had the final say, turned it down, and a great opportunity was lost. However, Central Mining was not alone among mining houses in regarding the venture as highly speculative, and the group's Consulting Geologist, Dr E.T. Mellor, influenced by the knowledge of earlier failures in the area, submitted an unfavourable opinion. It was left to Sir Abe Bailey, General Mining, and Anglo American, newest of the groups and struggling for survival, to join Gold Fields. F.A. Unger, Manager and Consulting Engineer of Anglo American, described the venture as a 'gamble'. It was however 'certainly a very attractive one and of a type in which a mining house is absolutely justified in risking even a considerable sum of money'. It was not long before it was apparent that the long shot was a winner. No less than 21 of the boreholes sunk as Krahmann indicated intersected highly payable reef.

Stokes was soon busily looking for ways to recover the lost opportunity, and to enable Rand Mines to obtain an interest in an area of which John A. Agnew, Gold Fields' Chairman, permitted himself to say guardedly:

I find it difficult to avoid extravagant language in outlining the possibilities.

Stokes, the hunter's instincts aroused, found a strip of land not taken up by Gold Fields on the farm Blyvooruitzicht, and bullied the directors of Central Mining into acquiring the right to mine it. He then applied all his diplomacy in negotiation with Gold Fields who generously allocated a much larger surrounding area, to enable Rand Mines to establish a viable mining proposition. A single borehole was sunk on the property, and on the evidence of this, and of boreholes sunk on other properties, the decision was taken to establish the Blyvooruitzicht mine. Stokes was appointed Chairman of the Company. The richness of its reefs exceeded all expectations. An unsuspected reef, to be known as the Carbon Leader, displaying visible gold, was found to underlie the property. Blyvooruitzicht became the wonder mine of the age until at last overtaken by neighbouring West Driefontein.

Thus, 1937 was a significant year for a young mining engineer to spend a term at head office observing at first hand the unfolding of great events. Hill worked closely with Walton and Stokes who continuously called for reports from him on diverse aspects of starting the new mine. He was set to work planning surface and underground layouts. There were decisions to be taken about shaft locations, the programming of water and power reticulation, and the siting of installations. He was allowed a big say in the layout of the mine, though naturally he did not always get his way.

> I admired Walton greatly — a charming man and a real English gentleman; but alas! We did not see eye-to-eye on the provision of amenities. There was a farmhouse on the mine surrounded by beautiful trees and I said to Walton, 'I think this is where the manager should live.' His reply was, 'No! no! no! The manager should live where he can look out of the windows and see whether or not the wheels in the headgear are turning.'
>
> He gave me the impression that living conditions on the mine should not be soft. He told me, 'You know when I started a coal mine in the UK we had a bed in the kitchen which we folded back to the wall every morning'. Many of the proposals I put forward for making home life on the mines pleasant and agreeable were found too advanced and too expensive.

As development of the first mines on the Far West Rand got underway, the attention of the mining houses was directed further west and south of the Vaal. As long ago as 1902 a Committee of Consulting Engineers appointed by the Chamber of Mines had reported indications that there was a 500 km Golden Arc which would one day be mined across the Far West Rand and through Klerksdorp into the Orange Free State. As the years of peace ran out in the 1930s, drilling programmes multiplied and the store of geophysical knowledge mounted. Then in April 1939 a borehole drilled by Western Holdings in the Free State struck the Basal Reef at 348 metres yielding a core projecting a level of payability 15 times the minimum needed to launch a mine at that time. The mining houses would soon be sure that a great new gold-field had been discovered, but the outbreak of war halted the race for a share in its riches.

By then Hill had completed his attachment at Rand Mines head office. He left in July 1939, armed with a wealth of new experience, to take up the toughest, and ultimately the most rewarding assignment of his career, the management of a section of the ultra-deep East Rand Proprietary Mines.

CHAPTER THREE

It's a Battlefield

When Hill took over as Manager of the Central Section of the ERPM he faced a situation altogether different from his previous mining experience.

> I encountered for the first time the 'battlefield' of an ultra-deep mine ... it meant a constant waging of war against pressure and heat.

ERPM was blasting out gold-bearing rock below 5 000 feet, and enduring its full share of the scourge of deep-level mining — rockbursts, sometimes of disruptive force, exploding without warning from the enormous pressure of the overhanging rock mass. It was enduring as well the ventilation problems encountered in old mines as they thrust deeper, an atmosphere so hot and humid that some miners dubbed it 'the dragon's breath'. It was a fantastic change from the relatively pleasant environment of the New Modder which seemed in retrospect 'factory-like'. Sharing the experience with war-time mining students at Wits, Hill declared:

> Overcoming heat and pressure, or minimizing their effect is a constant challenge to the mining engineer's intelligence and courage. In deep mines you are not tilting at windmills — you are grappling with grim realities, and

successes attained give a feeling of deep satisfaction. Any contribution you may make makes the lives of thousands of underground workers a little less arduous, trying or dangerous.

Two months after Hill's arrival at ERPM, South Africa declared war on Germany. Gold mining was declared to be an essential service, providing the sinews of war. It was given priority in materials, and its employees were declared to be 'key men' and barred from volunteering for military service. Nevertheless mining companies were at once confronted with demands from employees to be allowed to volunteer, and as many as possible were released, compatible with the maintenance of gold production.

Remarkably, gold output rose for the first three years of the war, and did not fall below the 1938 level in 1943–45. But the absence of mining men released for service added to the burdens of those who remained. Despite this many mining employees, including Hill who was very much a key man, served in the Mines Engineering Brigade, a voluntary part-time unit formed for home defence. A comrade-at-arms remembers Hill as 'the serjeant-major's nightmare — crumpled uniform and a sloppy salute'. Nonetheless Hill rose to command an artillery unit with the rank of captain, and found in it a happy diversion from the unceasing demands of management — and some unexpected military aptitude.

In camp at Potchefstroom he was required to direct a battery shoot against a target 2 000 metres away, from a vantage point on a kopje. The procedure was to call the estimated range, mark where the shells fell and give the necessary correction. One hoped that after further ranging shots and further corrections, a satisfactory straddle would be achieved, so that fire could then be directed to hit the target. It happened otherwise with Hill:

> I gave my first order and the shells fell dead on the target, first salvo. I was henceforth known as 'one-shot Pinkie'.

The comradeship and good fun of part-time military service provided only brief breaks from Hill's private war with the forces of nature at ERPM. The mine had its origins in the late 19th Century, but had been re-structured in 1909, incorporating six mining companies. For many years it was the largest gold mine in the world. Corner House, as the Central Mining/Rand Mines Group has been popularly known since pioneer days, took over the property after the death in 1914 of the founder Randlord, Sir George Farrar. The conglomerate which would include the Angelo, Angelo Reef, Cinderella, Cason, New Comet, New Blue Sky and Doornfontein Mines, proved a major disappointment. In the 15 years between 1917 and 1931 the mine only once paid a dividend, and its closure was contemplated.

The mine was not only the most extensive in the world; it was the deepest as well. Modern mines are planned in advance to minimize the effects of the massive rock pressures likely to be encountered, and to ensure adequate ventilation of the deepest levels. Not so ERPM in 1939; it had 'grown like Topsy'. It was a complex of old mine workings beginning at or near the outcrop and probing downwards. These were divided into three main sections, Central, East and West. Central, which Hill took over, was the richest and the deepest. Though the sections operated under a single overall management, and were connected underground, in practical terms they were really quite separate.

Shaft systems inherited from early days saddled successive managers with the problem of ventilating the huge workings through shafts that were poorly placed and inadequate in size for the volumes of air required. Large new inclines were sunk as the mine increased in depth, but for many years the handicap remained — the first shafts from the surface were bottlenecks and totally inadequate.

The fortunes of ERPM, like those of other mines, were transformed when South Africa went off the Gold Standard in December 1932. The value of its ore reserves doubled overnight, in accordance with the higher gold price, and it became the most profitable in the Corner House stable. Funds became available for much needed capital works and by 1938 three new vertical shafts had been completed, and a refrigeration plant for cooling mine air had been approved. However when Hill arrived in 1939 he found that the heat in the stopes was producing cases of heat stroke which were occasionally fatal, while the capacity of miners for physical exertion was fast dissipated. He grasped the opportunity the new shaft system offered to re-structure the distribution of air to the working faces.

Hill was faced too with an accident fatality rate around three times the modern norm in the industry, largely as a result of rockfalls and rockbursts. The frequency of rockbursts, increasing with depth, had reached the stage where management knew that it could expect three or four rockbursts a month; and that if they were severe and occurred during the shift where men were working, death and injury would result.

There is a tendency for bursts to be triggered by blasting at the shift end, and to occur when the workforce has left the mine; but even if men escape injury a severe burst can present the incoming shift with a demoralizing scene of devastated stopes and tunnels, and smashed equipment. Because pressure and heat increase as mining proceeds downward Hill judged that conditions were approaching the limits of human tolerance.

Dora Hill recalls:

> When my husband went to ERPM we carried on living for a time in our house at New Modder. Francis used to come home at night appalled at what was happening. The old hands just shrugged and said: 'That's how it is at ERPM'. But Francis wouldn't accept it. Although he never showed it he was a very sensitive man.
>
> Francis was fortunate in the managers he worked under. At New Modder there was Meyer, an enlightened pioneer of scientific management. At ERPM the General Manager, A.H. Krynauw, was happy to give Francis a free hand to get on with things.

But getting on with things was not to prove easy at all. Officials with mining degrees were rare in those days, but there was one in Ken E. Steele. He remembers Hill as a slight, unassuming figure, looking 'incredibly boyish'. Once visiting a shaft at night, Hill was greeted by the man in charge with 'Run off, Sonny — can't you see I'm busy!' The men he had working for him were tough and, Steele apart, self-made men who had risen from the ranks, with a *skiet-en-donder* attitude. They didn't think much at first of this upstart graduate fellow. But they underwent an abrupt change of attitude as Hill stood past practice on its ears. Steele paints a vivid picture of ERPM in those early days.

> ERPM was an extremely difficult mine because of great depth. Many pressure bursts occurred and the mine was unpopular. The complement of Black labourers was only kept up by drafting in new recruits. Productivity was low. The ventilation was ghastly, mainly as a result of poor return airways. The system of scattered mining was leaving remnants, a main cause of rockbursts. Hill

stopped all mining in the deeper levels to concentrate on dealing with the problem. He made me his personal assistant with the title of Remnant Officer. It was my duty to visit the scene of every burst and to make proper record. It was hazardous. The air was bad because the fall of rock disrupted ventilation. I was twice carried unconscious from such places, once regaining consciousness in hospital.

Steele adds:

Hill approached *every* activity from the scientific point of view. Fuses, drill steels, shovels — nothing escaped his attention in the search for greater efficiency and productivity. His code was: first, research the problem; then, define causes; arrive at a solution; develop standard procedures; control by meticulous application of standards.

Somehow Hill found time to observe that labourers' shovels, employed in huge numbers, wore down fast in the shovelling of abrasive quartzitic rock. And that when wear went beyond a certain stage it reduced the load of rock a labourer could lift, and his productivity. He had the miners' shovel redesigned with a hole in it to show when it had reached an unproductive stage of wear. Years later when asked why he had been given a high honour for his contribution to the advance of science, he replied: 'I got it for putting a hole in a shovel'.

But there were much more critical challenges at ERPM. Soon after his arrival Hill sent a formal report to Krynauw, emphasizing the unsatisfactory working environment arising from excessive heat and bursts in stopes, drives and haulages. He pointed out that while the new ventilation scheme and refrigeration plant, soon to come into operation, would enhance the quality of mine air, certain important areas would be little improved unless more labour was employed on opening up return airways.

He put forward a comprehensive list of improvements that would be necessary as well to control pressure bursts. He asked for an increase of 800 in the labour force. This labour would be unproductive, but it would create conditions in which future work could be carried out more efficiently and safely. If it were not forthcoming, he could see little prospect of reducing accidents, effectively cooling the working places, or avoiding production losses.

Rockbursts are defined by scientists as the 'uncontrolled disruption of rock associated with a violent release of energy'. They are characterized as seismic events and though of far less magnitude, have a lot in common with earthquakes. Both phenomena involve the release of seismic energy caused by the relative movements of rock masses, mostly on existing geological discontinuities. Rockbursts usually have magnitudes of less than 4 on the Richter scale, but magnitudes as high as 5,2 have been recorded.

Rockbursts occur in deep mining everywhere in the world without warning, and usually result in a tremor felt on the surface. They can vary from the unimportant in terms of danger or damage to the destructive and lethal. South African mines are especially afflicted because of the great depths achieved. The nature of the rock plays its part too, the hard, brittle quartzites of the Rand being peculiarly liable to energy overload and violent fracture.

Bursts may occur in shallow workings, but since the pressure in rock depends mainly on the weight of the overlying strata, the greater the depth the greater the pressure and, therefore, the greater the tendency for rockbursts to occur as mining proceeds downward. Mines in which a high percentage of ore is payable may be especially liable. If 90 per cent of the ore is payable and extracted, then the overlying strata eventually rests on only 10 per cent of intact ground, and the pressure will be much greater than if the intact or unmined ground were, say, 50 per cent of the total. The presence of faults (displacement of strata) or dykes (extrusions of volcanic rock) also play their part. The rock adjoining them will tend to be more highly stressed. Hill found that the incidence of bursts near faults and dykes was several times greater then in normal undisturbed ground.

Violent collapse of underground workings has long posed a serious problem to miners. Possibly the earliest recorded incident was the catastrophic collapse of the old tin workings at Altenberg, Saxony, in 1640 which caused a tremor felt in Dresden 30 miles to the north. In South Africa the problem has been increasingly serious ever since mines began probing deeper levels. In 1908 the Ophirton Earth Tremors Committee carried out an investigation, resulting in the setting up of a seismic station at the Union Observatory in Johannesburg. By 1918 it was recording an average of 200 tremors a year. There were other official enquiries in 1915 and 1924. The problem became ever-more critical as mines went deeper.

By the thirties the avoidance of rockbursts had become a regular subject of discussion and debate at the meetings of the Association of Mine Managers, and important, and imaginative, individual contributions were made. Miners, too, became increasingly aware of stress build up in the rock around them. The deeper working places would creak and murmur. The men would say 'the rock is talking' and would try to draw on experience to judge whether the 'talk' meant a beneficial release of stress by the fracturing of rock behind the face, or whether it indicated an impending rockfall or burst. Today 'rocktalk' is scientifically recorded and dignified with the designation of 'micro-seismic event'.

By 1939, although mining engineers had made advances in the avoidance of rockbursts derived from observation and experience, there was little scientific knowledge of their cause or nature. Because of this relative ignorance of the forces at play, the methods evolved for the control of ground lacked the certainty of a scientific base. Moreover, because mines and their problems are as varied as human fingerprints, there was a considerable difference in approach, and no method of general application emerged, while the problems increased in complexity.

It was typical of Hill's innovative turn of mind that he perceived that a radical change in the system of mining at ERPM could reduce the situations in which rock stress reached bursting point; and would permit an equally radical improvement in the ventilation of working places.

Hill's solution was a move from the system of scattered stoping to a system in which mining was concentrated on longwall faces, on a scale new to gold mining. In the 'scattered system' then in general use, the ore was exposed by means of tunnels in the plane of the reef, the ore body being divided into blocks of ground. The result of this method was the subsequent creation of 'island abutments' or remnants, each of which was liable to burst several times because of the excessively high stresses that developed in small pillars of unmined ground.

Hill perceived that by concentrating mining in longwalls, the formation of remnants could be largely eliminated, and the incidence of rockbursts reduced because fewer areas would be subjected to excessive stress concentration.

Coincident with the phased introduction of longwall faces, Hill introduced additional support systems. No support system then available could resist the explosive thrust of a burst, but it could prevent rockfalls arising from a simple break in the strata. On 22 May, 1942 he presented the results to the Association of Mine Managers in a paper entitled 'an experiment in support at depth at the East Rand Proprietary Mines, Ltd', the first of more than 100 papers, addresses and contributions to local and overseas societies, institutes and congresses.

Hill's successful concentration on methods of countering heat and pressure throughout his six years at ERPM, and later as a consulting engineer, would provide guidelines for the multi-disciplinary approach of the industry today in working 800 km of stope face and thousands of kilometres of shafts and tunnels at unprecedented depths.

CHAPTER FOUR

The Road Away From Hell

The innovation of large-scale longwall mining permitted not only the concentration of mining with a lower incidence of rockbursts, but a parallel concentration of ventilation. Man has to live and work within well-defined limits of body temperature. Normal temperature lies roughly between 36 and 36,9 degrees Celsius, but it may rise above 38 degrees in illness. At about 41 degrees life is endangered. Men performing manual labour in high temperatures may be similarly threatened.

A man at work is creating calories which heat his body and unless the environment is such that excess heat is quickly removed, he may collapse from heat stroke and die. It is obviously of prime importance for the worker's well-being, and his capacity to work, that he be efficiently cooled; and this can best be done by air that is cool, dry and moving.

In deep-level mining these requirements are not easily met, for the ventilating air in its passage to depth is heated by compression, and by the flow of heat from rock to air. In the deepest mines the rock may become hot to the touch, the so-called geothermic gradient varying with location and rock formation.

On the Kolar gold-fields of India men seem to be able to work in temperatures of as much as 50 degrees C, but the air is dry. On the Rand the mining engineer necessarily

43

chooses the lesser of two evils. The stopes are continually 'wetted down' to allay quartzitic dust and reduce the risks of miners' contracting silicosis. This essential practice ensures excess humidity. Temperatures of stopes are measured in so-called 'wet bulb' that indicates both temperature and the water content of the air. The greater the wet bulb temperature the less the cooling power of the air. It had been established by two distinguished mine medical officers, A.J. Orenstein and L.G. Irvine, as far back as 1921 that in humid air with a wet bulb temperature of 93 degrees F (33,8 C) and air velocity of 100 feet (30,48m) a minute, a man's capacity to work is cut by half. If the man worked harder in these conditions of heat and humidity he would become exhausted, his body temperature would rise and he would be exposed to the danger of heat stroke.

Half a century later the great scientist, Dr Austin Whillier, declared that the wet-bulb temperatures of 28 and 32 C defined the extremes of Heaven and Hell underground. As Whillier guided the industry further along 'the road away from Hell' he doffed his hat to Hill's pioneering role.

After introducing his new and radical approach at ERPM, Hill was enabled to report success to the Chemical, Metallurgical and Mining Society in September 1943 in 'A major changeover in the ventilation of a deep-level mine', a paper presented jointly with E.C. Ranson, the mine's Ventilation Officer. For this they were awarded the Society's Gold Medal, given for outstanding presentations of new expertise.

Hill told the Society that his objective at ERPM had been to ensure that not only should the quantities of air pumped underground be adequate, they should be coursed along the working faces with sufficient velocity to ensure cooling of body temperature by rapid evaporation of perspiration. The main feature of the new system was the high degree of control over the airflow by suitably placed ventilation doors, regulators and barriers; and the installation of a series of exhaust fans underground to give the required distribution, the volumes of air delivered being varied as required by adjustment to the fans. Fast-moving air, chilled in the surface refrigeration plant, was ducted to the area where men were engaged in manual labour.

He demonstrated that the benefits to the mine had been substantial. They included a greatly improved working environment; and a decrease in the incidence of heat stroke, accidents and sickness. The new scheme had increased enormously the volumes of air delivered to men at work and emphasized the value of maximum exploitation of air movement in cooling men in deep, hot places.

Hill introduced his paper by saying:

> Those of us entrusted with the task of extracting ore from great depths will always be faced with this problem — how to improve the ventilation of our working areas so as to overcome the effects of ever-increasing rock temperature. The answer we know is to concentrate the work, supply large volumes of air, concentrate the flow, control the flow.
>
> The methods of putting this principle into practise may vary. We have described the methods adopted on the ERPM — the results obtained have been most satisfactory and a new vista has opened before us. We are very optimistic.

Hill signposted future industry practice by asserting:

> In deep-level mining the planning of shafts, haulages and methods of mining must be governed largely by ventilation requirements.

Not every innovation worked out. Across ten days in March 1942 Hill carried out the experiment of cooling men by fitting them with ice-packs. Hill made himself chief guinea pig, together with two mine captains and two shift bosses. To determine the effect of wearing the ice-pack on rise of body temperature a tough underground course was chosen of about 1 400 metres of which 300 metres was uphill, 150 metres downhill, and 1 000 metres level. The course was covered in about two hours. Each of the five officials covered the course twice, walking in the drives and crawling in hot stopes, once with and once without the ice-pack some days apart.

The ice bag of about 1½ kg of crushed ice was strapped to the back against the bare flesh, but — by mining standards — it was not markedly uncomfortable. At the end of the test period the ice had all melted.

> I thought this would be a way to reduce body temperature! We five put the ice-packs on our backs and did the walk through particularly hot areas, our temperatures being recorded every half hour. Funnily enough, physiologically, I don't seem to react to heat as badly as other people. My temperature went up significantly less than that of the other four. The General Manager's comment was: 'Well, obviously you were born in Hell'. Alas! The tests were not very successful; we repeated the tour without ice-packs and found that their effect was only to decrease the rise in body temperature by about 0.25 per cent.

Hill's temperature without ice-pack was in fact lower than the senior mine captain's wearing the ice-pack. In later years scientific tests by mining industry physiologists would confirm that Hill was exceptionally heat tolerant.

The unsuccessful experiments pre-dated by about 30 years sophisticated experiments with ice-jackets carried out by Chamber of Mines research scientists — which did not produce results of general application either.

By 1944, Hill was able to report the success of the longwall system to the Association of Mine Managers in a paper entitled 'A system of longwall stoping in a deep-level mine, with special reference to its bearing on pressure burst and ventilation problems'. He declared, with prescience, that:

> In the mines of the Central Witwatersrand where payability is over 65 per cent, some form of longwall stoping will be necessary at depths below 8 500 feet.
>
> One of the main objects of this paper will be to show why this belief is held and more particularly why longwall stoping seems so significant a pointer towards a solution of the serious heat and pressure problems that will have to be faced in the ultra-deep level mines of the future.

Hill reported that he had introduced longwall stoping with the primary object of lessening the number of pressure bursts. There had been a most gratifying reduction in their number and severity. In 1941, 1942 and 1943 the Central Section suffered respectively, 156, 79 and 55 bursts, the progressive decline being attributed directly to the introduction of longwalling and the consequent elimination of remnants.

All pressure phenomena were recorded and discussed at monthly meetings. To be recorded as a pressure burst, the event had to cause enough damage to delay work for at least a shift; and not be only a fall of ground — the hanging, footwall or face had to have burst — to have been thrust with force into the excavation. 'Talking' of the rock in stopes, small bursts and falls of ground were not classed as pressure bursts.

> We try to remove from the minds of officials, miners and natives the great nervous strain that is present when stopes and drives are continually bursting, and our main concern is for the safety of places where men are actually at work.

Hill emphasized the danger of forming remnants:

> The evil of bursts in remnants is still very much with us and the time seems propitious to deliver an attack against any policy which tolerates the formation of remnants in areas subject to pressure bursting. If ERPM experience is a true guide, it is impossible to prevent pressure bursting in remnants. Intensive support, rapid advance, attention to shape of remnant and direction of face advance — all these and combinations of these have been tried in vain.

Apart from the considerable diminution in pressure bursts, the advantages of longwall mining included more standard conditions, and better organisational control. Work had been concentrated. Ventilation had improved considerably, the number of heat stroke cases falling from six a year to one in 1943. Supervision was easier, and so was sampling and surveying. Production had increased as well as the scope for mechanization. There had even been a reduction in mining costs.

However, the problem of rockbursts had been alleviated, not solved. ERPM continued to suffer from them. They remain today the major hazard of mining at ultra-deep levels compounded as mines thrust ever deeper into the earth's crust. But an advance had been made in their control which would influence mining decisions in all the years to come.

Hill recognised that longwalling would not be applicable to all mining situations. Concentrated mining of the large area of ground involved in a longwall stope made the control of grade more difficult. The average grade of ore mined would tend to be less than with a more selective system. In other words some sacrifice of profit was involved. He foresaw correctly that longwalling would become a standard stoping method in ultra-deep mines, and that the sacrifices of profit involved would be accepted.

In 1946 Hill was promoted to General Manager of Durban Deep, the Corner House gold mine just west of Johannesburg. His years at ERPM had been tough, but because so much could be achieved he had fully enjoyed them.

Nothing ever gave him greater satisfaction than the knowledge that the toll of lives had been reduced. There was the satisfaction, too, of knowing that a more acceptable working environment had been created.

In addition to heat and pressure, there had been all the usual preoccupations of management, some dramatic. For example:

> While I was at ERPM, a fire broke out in the stopes on the western side of the mine; it arose near a sub-incline shaft, and the depth was about 6 000 feet. A fire-fighting office was established at the top of the shaft. Tackling the fire were Proto teams on each level; while these efforts were being made, the main ventilating fan cut out, and the downcast current reversed and smoke started pouring into the incline shaft. Fortunately, an electrician realized what had happened, raced along the haulage, and restarted the nearby fan; the current was reversed, and

smoke and gas cleared, and the danger of gassing the workers at the top of the incline shaft had passed.

An amusing incident occurred shortly after the fire broke out. The eastern flank of the fire area was being patrolled by two men carrying a canary in a cage in order to detect the presence or otherwise of carbon monoxide. One of the men obviously did not know why they were carrying the canary because, when it dropped off its perch, he said, 'Say mate, they've given us a sick canary.'.

Another event produced an illuminating sidelight on Hill's managerial stance.

A fire broke out in the mine, and after it was quelled, we feared a further flare up and posted men at strategic points to watch through the night for any signs of smoke. Fire did break out, and the man who should have reported it had fallen asleep at his post. It spread considerably before being spotted. That was about the only time in my life I ever fired a man. It would have been very bad for the general discipline of the mine to overlook the matter. I felt so damn sorry for him.

Clearly, Hill was a new breed of manager, wholly unlike some of those who held sway over mines in the past. There was nothing in him of the manager who, so the story goes, telephoned the mine police in the night and commanded them to silence a cricket in his garden. During the course of Hill's mining career there were those who took advantage of his natural kindness. 'In America', commented his friend Syd Newman, 'he would have been a gift for a con man'. But at ERPM he proved that the quiet personality and the boyish appearance concealed an iron will; and that he could not only conceive imaginative solutions, but inspire others to carry them through to finality. With such men he forged an enduring bond. One of them was Ken Steele.

In 1964 after varied mining experience, Steele would return to ERPM as General Manager. Hill wrote to congratulate him on 8 May of that year:

> When you and I were there about 25 years ago we began studying problems of heat and pressure; some advance was made but alas these intractable problems are still very much with us and you will find them the major challenge .... .

Steele, who was himself to make a significant contribution at ERPM to the problems of heat and pressure, replied:

> Well do I remember your grappling with the problems. But for your success in these matters who knows but that ERPM might not have been in existence today. I often wonder just how many people realise or appreciate this fact.

CHAPTER FIVE

Manager, New Style

In 1945, a young man named Reinald Hofmeyr had just returned from university and military service when he heard that an unusual job was going at the Durban Deep gold mine.

> I had grown up in Pretoria where the knowledge of mines and mining was minimal. When I decided to follow up this job, one of the things that attracted me was the word Durban because I had always liked the idea of working at the coast.

He had yet to find out that the full name of the mine was The Durban Roodepoort Deep Gold Mining Company Ltd, situated west of Johannesburg, and financed by a group of Durban businessmen in the pioneer days.

> The fact that it turned out to be at Roodepoort didn't really matter because Pinkie made the job sound so interesting that I accepted without delay.

After his travels in Europe and America 15 years before Hill had resolved that as soon as he was promoted to mine manager and had the power to do so he would set up a personnel department to bring expert knowledge to bear on human problems. At Durban Deep he at once made his pioneering dream a reality, at a time when the normal problems of industrial relations were complicated by a special need — to ensure that the men who had been fighting in Africa and Europe got a square deal on their return to mine employment.

Hill had previously set up an employment office at New Modder, but it was limited in scope. Now he established a personnel department covering recruitment, selection, some training, welfare, employee counselling and other aspects of industrial relations. Personnel management in Britain and the United States had grown impressively under war-time conditions. In South Africa it had made a modest start in commerce and industry, but had not yet appeared on the mines where management's relations with skilled and supervisory staff, then almost entirely White, were sometimes abysmal. Hill, an exceptional judge of men, saw in Reinald Hofmeyr a man of the right quality with the essential fundamental interest in his fellow man. He groomed him carefully for the role.

Hofmeyr recalls:

> Before I was allowed to begin, Pinkie insisted that I attend a course in personnel management at Rhodes University under Isabel White who had pioneered personnel management in the Eastern Cape. This lasted for six months and I then started at Durban Deep in July 1946. My training continued however because Pinkie had arranged a programme to familiarize me with the work in every department of the mine. This included 110 underground shifts, and by the time I was transferred to Rand Mines head office in 1955 I had clocked up over 500 underground shifts. I sometimes wonder how many youngsters entering personnel management today are subjected to the same rigorous induction.

The first major objective set the department was to reduce the turnover of supervisory and skilled employees, running at 70 per cent a year, a rate then not uncommon in the mining industry. That figure would be cut to 40 per cent in two years. This was achieved, firstly, by so-called 'exit interviews', in which each departing employee was interviewed, and asked why he was leaving. Then monthly meetings were held at which each resignation or dismissal was discussed. Detailed records were kept which showed up the departments with high staff turnover; monthly reviews highlighted bad working conditions, or personalities causing friction with fellow workers. It was then up to those responsible to set about improving the situation.

Hill got across to officials the concept, novel to some, that top management cared about its workforce and that, moreover, the resignation of a worker represented a financial loss to the company in training a replacement and making him familiar with the section of the mine he was to supervise or work in. He inculcated the realisation that firing a man was not something to be done lightly, because the loss of employment could be catastrophic for the man concerned and costly to the company. The main aim was firmly declared — a contented labour force, a body of employees who would put their hearts into their work, and enjoy security of employment for as long as they did.

Hofmeyr's early days were not easy.

Many mine officials and a number of mine managers regarded a personnel department as some new-fangled nonsense for which there was really no call, but Pinkie's belief in it, and support for it, were unwavering. One of the most sceptical was the mine secretary at Durban Deep, V.J. Pickerill, a good friend of mine who undoubtedly had my best interests at heart as he saw them. Pickerill assured me that there was no future in the mining industry for personnel management and advised me to join something like the O.K. Bazaars. I am glad I never took his advice because I certainly had a very full and rewarding career.

As personnel management took hold in Rand Mines under Hill's urging and example, and spread to the whole mining industry, Hofmeyer would become Group Personnel Manager at Rand Mines head office with alternate director status, and go on to become an Executive Director of Barlow Rand, responsible for both personnel management and industrial relations in that huge conglomerate. His appointment at Durban Deep was the beginning of a long association with Hill and a mutually supportive friendship. He recalls:

> One of Pinkie's great strengths was that he was an innovator in so many fields. He was the father of personnel management, he really gave an enormous impetus to what we now call environmental control, to work study, rock mechanics and mining research. He is of course a most remarkable, modest and lovable character. He is one of the most lucid people in both speaking and writing. If there is a flaw, it is, I believe, that he is so generous of mind as to refuse to believe ill of anybody; and I do think that this made it difficult for him to make some of the harsh decisions which have to be taken in the business world...

Once having established personnel management at Durban Deep Hill became a prime mover in the wider propagation of the need for an approach to the handling of personnel that was both scientific and humane. In 1946 he helped to found the Johannesburg branch of the Institute of Personnel Management, with 60 members, and became its first chairman.

In his report to the Transvaal branch on the first year of its existence, Hill declared:

> We are slowly realising that man is more important than the machine. Personnel management aims simply at bringing greater knowledge and understanding to bear on human problems ... Production in industry is not so much a question of technical equipment as it is of getting human beings to pull together. Our immediate problem is a human problem. How can greater co-operation be achieved? How can employees be given more satisfaction in their work which will make the industrial machine run more smoothly? Certainly not by authority blinding itself to the demands or wishes of employees, or by the use of force.

A year later he reported that personnel management had gained a firm footing in Britain and the United States, and had clearly come to stay in those countries. In South Africa personnel management was still a 'Cinderella'. He forecast however that in 20 years it would have won general acceptance in the larger industries. But he feared growth would be painfully slow, for the opposition was strong, the greatest resistance coming from older men in executive positions.

Hill had already run head-on into conflict with some of his fellow managers on the value of personnel management and the necessity for it on the gold mines. In the last days of the War the Chamber of Mines formed an advisory body on social services and gave it the initial role of helping to find suitable employment for returned soldiers, many of whom had left lowly jobs on the mines and progressed to positions of responsibility in the armed forces. Hill grasped the opportunity to urge on the Association of Mine Managers that the establishment of personnel departments was the only way to ensure skilled attention to the problem, and effective liaison between mine and Chamber. He ventured further, into the fields of recruitment, education and promotion. The system of recruitment, he declared, was lacking in method and men were being signed on because they were the best on offer, rather than the best qualified. Young men in mining jobs were being given little encouragement to fit themselves for higher responsibility by further education. Moreover, promotion and transfer seemed to operate largely on chance. A manager could never feel sure that promotion would be given to the man who most deserved it.

At the Association meeting, held on 22 June, 1945, another lively manager, J.S. Ford, backed him up, praising Hill's restraint of language in pointing out profound weaknesses. He declared: 'Recruitment is haphazard, education, promotion and transfer are all haphazard.' There were others who supported him as well. However there were authoritarian managers of a breed then already passing from the scene, men who by hard driving had seen the industry through tough days in the past. These were complacent in their confidence that the standard reached by the social services was of the highest order, and required no pseudo-scientific system or presumptuous under-managers to improve.

Hill, while admitting that a great deal was done to provide amenities and good, safe working conditions, crossed swords with those who claimed that all was well in the field of human relationships. He told the Association:

How can all be well when there are such widespread

feelings of insecurity, when most employees are treated as productive units rather than human beings, and when so many work on the mines because they have no alternative? I fully agree that senior officials may have qualities of tact, sympathy, self-control and understanding of human nature ... A cornerstone in my argument is that senior executives, no matter how fitted or gifted in the handling of human problems, cannot do justice to this portion of their work because they do not have the time.

There were those with reasonable doubts and more reasoned argument against the introduction of a new division of management. The distinction between line management and personnel management is a fine one, the personnel official being there to advise and not usurp nor intrude on the province of executive management. In the mining industry where delegation of responsibility and legal liability tend to go hand in hand, the definition of the separate function, and the careful choice of the right men for the personnel job, was to be all-important.

These were problems requiring to be resolved in the light of practical experience, but Hill was tireless in expounding the principles involved, and the advantages that must flow from their proper application. In 1948, at the age of 42 his status as a rising star in the mining industry would be recognised by his contemporaries by his election to the presidency of the premier professional society in mining, the Chemical, Metallurgical and Mining Society of South Africa (now the S.A. Institute of Mining and Metallurgy). He had declined nomination as President a year earlier, but accepted the vice-presidency. Hill chose as the theme of his presidential address another subject dear to his heart 'Management in Industry', and argued eloquently about the need to train managers. He pointed out that the USA with seven per cent of the world's population was producing 40 per cent of the world's wealth. Her population produced nine times per head more than the other people of the world.

America's great natural resources played an important role, but it was mainly the American genius for industry that made the standard of living of her people so incomparably high. In this great achievement a factor of far-reaching importance was the efficiency of management, and this in turn flowed from comprehensive management training, at the time almost wholly lacking in South Africa.

In a detailed survey of each function of management Hill seized the opportunity to break a lance for specialization in personnel.

No specialist department of management, he said, had been so misunderstood and so suspiciously received as the personnel department.

> Perhaps this is because ... its activities reach into all the branches of a business, and because all supervisors feel that the handling of employees is peculiarly personal and no part of it can be delegated to a specialist. To prevent discord a manager must show why these suspicions and fears are groundless and why if personnel management is properly understood and applied, it adds considerably to the well-being of employees and the general efficiency and morale in an organization.
>
> ... a personnel department's basic nature is that of a service department, ancillary and advisory in scope and existing primarily to help the executive staff in dealing more efficiently with their human problems ... The department supplies the management with those facts which will throw a clearer light on the employees in an organization.

On the broader theme of scientific management Hill expressed the credo grown out of study and reflection since leaving Oxford. The manager must inculcate in his staff the scientific state of mind, for without this no great progress was possible. The scientific mind was prepared to accept change. Most people however did not want change for this meant effort, bestirring themselves from the pleasant groove of known ways. Inherent in human beings was this reluctance to change. It required enthusiasm to overcome this apathy and to show that new knowledge was vital to industrial progress and, even, to survival.

Industry was concerned with materials, machines and men, and of these factors what mattered most was men. You could give a man a machine, but you couldn't make him work it well unless you motivated him strongly enough. Managers must ensure that financial rewards apart, workers were provided with an environment that was as healthy, clean and cheerful as possible. Supremely, the manager must have the human approach, the desire and capacity to see the other man's point of view. He must show sound judgment in selecting supervisory staff, for these were key men who could do so much to create congenial human relationships. The manager must provide for promotions on a basis of merit, and his decisions regarding personnel must bear the obvious stamp of justice.

> Above all, men must feel that they are human beings with desires and aspirations, not just tools to be coldly used and lightly discarded ... .
>
> To create an atmosphere in which men willingly give of their best — that is the ideal, unattainable because of man's imperfections, but an ideal that should surely be a beacon to those entrusted with the responsibilities of management.

Despite the initial scepticism about the need for personnel departments and considerable misunderstanding and antagonism, they multiplied in the mining industry from the late 1940s onward, until it became unthinkable to run a mine of any size without a well-staffed and competent personnel set-up contributing to the welfare and efficiency of the total labour force. And because commerce and industry tend to follow a lead from the mines, personnel management received a boost in all branches of economic activity. By 1960 the institute founded by Isabel White in Port Elizabeth and by Hill in Johannesburg had grown in membership and prestige to the stage where it was legally recognised as the Institute of Personnel Management (South Africa) and was accorded equal status with the other professional and scientific societies. Hill was the natural choice as its first president. Characteristically his presidential address was entitled 'Dynamic Administration' and paid tribute to an American pioneer in the field of scientific management, Mary Parker Follett. Her writings were described to Hill by Colonel L. Urwick, the doyen of British management consultants, as 'the product of a brilliant and vital mind which has immersed itself in the study of human relations'. She believed, said Hill, that the most important problems of an organization had a psychological basis: they stemmed from the interaction of individuals in the working group.

> ... I have been able to give only a few samples from the gold mine (of her work); but the samples are rich. Integration in preference to domination; the concept of participation; co-ordination from the bottom upwards; study of the total situation for effective control; 'power with' rather than 'power over'; the depersonalizing of orders; making conflict constructive; recognising that authority should rest with capacity and knowledge; thinking in

terms of group power rather than individual power.

Personnel management, and the Institute, would continue to grow until today the Institute which began post-war with a handful of members, has more than 10 000. In 1989 one thousand of them attended a convention at Sun City, and Hill, an honorary fellow of the Institute, was there by special invitation to receive a framed reproduction of the Institute's coat of arms.

Apart from pioneering personnel management, at Durban Deep Hill experienced a full share of the demands made on a general manager in meeting production targets, carrying out new development and introducing longwall mining to the extent that proved practical. He also introduced there an innovative method of shaft sinking. When a shaft was sunk it was customary to leave a large area of ground around it unmined to form a 'pillar' which would give the shaft stability. When the shaft was sunk through gold-bearing ground however the time came when operations contracted to the stage where it was desirable to mine the gold in the pillar. But the shaft pillar then constituted a remnant in largely mined-out ground and was subject to high pressure from overlying rock with a high incidence of rockbursts causing injury to workers and sometimes throwing the shaft out of alignment. Hill's pioneering idea was to remove the ground around the shaft as soon as the shaft was sunk and before mining started, thus taking advantage of the relative stability of the surrounding rock mass, while allowing the area to settle so that the shaft's stability would be established for its working life. Hill carried this out successfully at Durban Deep, as he would later at Harmony mine, making important investigations into the way in which rock masses settle after disturbance by excavation. Although the technique would be superseded as other approaches were introduced, Hill's experiments focused attention once again on the need to search out new ways to offset the toll of rockburst fatalities.

Despite his heavy managerial work load, Hill never deviated from his belief in the principle that a manager should be accessible to all.

Young W.P. 'Bob' Plewman, later Professor of Mining at Witwatersrand University, like Hill a Rhodes Scholar, went to Durban Deep as a student on vacation employment in 1946. Studying the mine plans Plewman was able to identify a deposit of Kimberley Reef in the Old Britannia Mine which had been incorporated in Durban Deep, and reported this to Hill. Hill took time to listen to his very young subordinate and acted with typical thoroughness. He sent for and studied the plans himself, then called for the responsible official and asked him for estimates of the time and cost involved in opening the necessary drive to the Kimberley Reef. Plewman recalls; 'He took an instant decision to go ahead with important results for the mine.'

Another view of Hill at Durban Deep was recorded by a brilliant Hungarian scientist, Mischi Barcza, who became Group Ventilation Officer of Rand Mines and later still Managing Director of Rand Mines Laboratories. He recalled:

> When I first met him on Durban Deep, where I was sent on temporary secondment for a special task, I had a unique experience. He was the first mine manager to ask me to sit down, to give me a cup of tea and to speak to me on an equal footing. The fact that such treatment by mine managers has become customary is in no small measure the result of Hill's example.

Hill recalls with pleasure an opportunity to brighten the environment. In those days mines were dreary places. Nobody bothered much to clear away disused machinery and piles of surplus material. As the years went by, the mine surface became a desert of crumbling buildings, rusting metal and discarded, rotting junk. Durban Deep was no exception. Dora Hill recalls: 'The mine when we arrived was like a scrap yard. Awful!' Hill set in train a monster clean-up.

Then came one of those times of drama that abound in mining. White miners throughout the industry embarked on a strike arising from a struggle for power within the Mineworkers' Union, and crippled the industry for a fortnight. The problem then arose for the mines of how to occupy the hundreds of thousands of Black miners who were not involved in the strike, but could not be legally taken underground without White supervisors. Hill's solution was to set his Black labour force of 8 000 men to planting trees. The countryside was scoured for plants and 10 000 of 20 varieties were planted on Durban Deep. Thereafter a man was employed solely to care for the young plants. As the years went by, Durban Deep was transformed into one of the pleasantest areas along the strike of the reef, and became a show mine to which it was customary to take the industry's most distinguished visitors. Forty years later Hill would still get pleasure from the tall trees that shaded the property. Hill saw too that land lying fallow was put to good use, and gave instructions for the cultivation on a huge scale of vegetable gardens to feed the men in the mine hostels.

The burdens of mine management are considerable, especially the unremitting responsibility for the safety and well-being of the many thousands employed continuously in an undertaking comprising a complexity of works and machinery, of deep-plunging shafts, haulage ways and stopes along the strike of the reef. The mine manager is required to live on the property and be on call 24 hours a day. Legal responsibility apart, it is the personality of the mine manager that quickens the corporate spirit through the disparate elements which combine in the most exacting of human tasks. Hill handled it all as though to the manner born:

> There is never a moment when the mine is out of mind, but I was never worried. I was concerned ... but it didn't worry me. There were many problems, tough problems. But, you know, when you see that there is something to be done about them — when you can evolve solutions, and bring them to fruition, that's exciting — gives great personal satisfaction.

As the immediate post-war years came to an end, and the ex-servicemen settled back to the works of peace, the mining industry geared up to exploit the vast potential of the new fields proved in the thirties. The new era of expansion that lay ahead would demand a more scientific approach to overcome heat and pressure, and other problems encountered at depth in the new fields; it would demand, too, a new concept and style of management to replace the out-dated authoritarian stance of the past. By 1947 Hill was recognised as the progressive scientific manager in the forefront of new thought. In April of that year he was appointed a Consulting Engineer to Rand Mines at the remarkably young age of 41. It was just 15 years since he had signed on as a greenhorn at New Modder. He was now ready to take a leading position among those who would evolve both a new technology, and a new humanitarian approach to the management of men.

CHAPTER SIX

Harmony and Some Discord

By 1947 it seemed that Corner House had lost out in the race for the riches of the Orange Free State. The discovery of the new gold-field ranked in importance with the previous great mineral discoveries in South Africa, that of the Kimberley diamond mines and the Witwatersrand gold-field. But while these two were found by accident or good fortune, the Free State gold-field was proven by the application of geological knowledge and theory, backed by the greatest drilling programme in the history of gold mining. That being said, there was a great deal of luck in the share-out of the bonanza. The outcome endorsed the credo of mining engineers that in mining enterprise fortune favours the brave.

In the Thirties and Forties every mining house on the Rand, as well as diverse companies and syndicates, took out options to mine on Free State farms. For years options were taken out, dropped and then taken up again by another company. Anglo American, Union Corporation, Western Holdings, and the African and European Investment Corporation, a Lewis and Marks subsidiary, carried out intensive drilling programmes. Other companies, sitting on options, watched and waited.

At the end of 1938, Anglo's first costly drilling programme had produced nothing. The Corporation was out of the Free State. A.P. Cartwright wrote in *Golden Age* that a poll of geologists and consulting engineers at that time would probably have shown, in aggregate, a conviction that payable gold would not be found.

The elusive Basal Reef, the principal gold-bearing deposit, was covered by the lava beds, up to 1 400 metres thick, that overlay much of the north-western Free State, and there were no surface signposts to the riches that lay far below. The magnetometer that had served so well on the West Wits Line was of little value in the virtual absence of magnetic strata. Union Corporation pioneered the torsion balance, a geophysical instrument that enabled geologists to plot the thickness of underlying lava or other strata, and to position boreholes on the most likely sites. The Corporation's geologists made a major contribution both to the strike by Western Holdings on the farm St Helena in 1939 and, overall, to picking the lock of the treasury of the Basal Reef.

Western Holdings belonged to Sir Abe Bailey's company, South African Townships. Sir Abe, who was nearing the end of his adventurous life, enjoyed friendly relations with the Corner House and suggested to John Martin that the Central Mining/Rand Mines Group take over his interests. Rand Mines however informed Central Mining in London that these were not worth taking over at the high price Sir Abe was asking. Sir Abe then let Martin know that if at any time the Corner House was interested, he would be happy to come to terms. He died in August 1940. His will named Martin as one of the executors, and it fell to him to find a purchaser for Sir Abe's companies.

Why did Martin not suggest that the Corner House take over Sir Abe's interests? Cartwright found:

> ... with his very high standard of business ethics, he would have regarded it as wrong to use his position as an

executor to sell assets to a company of which he was a director ... There was also the fact that Western Holdings was still a highly speculative venture and he was not a gambler. The strike at St Helena would not have made much difference to his estimate of the company's market value. In any case Central Mining held options on farms about five miles north of the St Helena borehole so he probably thought they were pretty close to the target anyway.

It was wartime and Martin found the Bailey interests hard to sell. The Johannesburg Consolidated Investment Company (JCI.) turned down the offer. Gold Fields was preoccupied with its own bonanza on the West Wits Line. It was left to Sir Ernest Oppenheimer of the Anglo American Corporation to see and grasp the opportunity to secure control of South African Townships and the controlling interest in Western Holdings. Sir Ernest said later, 'Anyone could have had control of Townships from the Trustees and for a very small outlay'. He followed up this key investment by obtaining control of African and European Investment Company which had important options on farms south of Odendaalsrus. Anglo was back in the Free State with a vengeance. From this firm base Sir Ernest moved to take a commanding position in the complexity of companies which held interests. As the full chart of the riches of the Free State unrolled, Anglo found itself in the million-pound seats. It would bring to production six large mines.

Mining houses traditionally compete fiercely for new mining propositions, and thereafter those who win them offer a piece of the action to those who do not, with hopes of a *quid pro quo* in time to come. But participation, however profitable, is never as attractive to mining entrepreneurs as effective control and the right of management. Thus though there was much inter-group co-operation in mobilizing the capital needed for shaft sinking and development of haulage ways, some of the mining houses would be left licking the wounds of might-have-been. Union Corporation, by its participation in Western Holdings, won the right to operate the first Free State mine, St Helena. But it had been otherwise out-manoeuvred so that it failed to realise fully on the achievements of its exploration teams. Gold Fields found it galling that properties controlled by other companies proved to be underlain by payable reef while their own no less energetic and scientifically-sound prospecting was unsuccessful. Corner House had the same sort of bad luck. The options which it had taken covered three blocks of farms near the village of Odendaalsrus. On information revealed by the boreholes available it was decided in 1940 to drop the options north and south of Odendaalsrus and hold those to the east.

Drilling began again as soon as the war was over, and 168 boreholes were sunk around Odendaalsrus. In April 1946, one of them, the Geduld Hole 1, showed the most spectacular result in mining history. When communicated privately to Anglo American head office the result was thought too good to be true, and it was feared that the sample had been salted. The Press too questioned the result, for nobody had ever heard of a borehole result of 23 037 inch-dwt (An inch-dwt being the width of a gold-bearing reef in inches multiplied by the assay value in pennyweights of gold per ton). The implications in terms of grade at the point where the drill penetrated the Basal Reef were staggering. On 25 April Sir Ernest told shareholders of the Orange Free State Investment Trust that it was now certain that a continuous gold-bearing area ran north and south of Odendaalsrus in which ten or eleven big gold mines would be established. By then the Johannesburg Stock Exchange was staging a boom in gold shares to match the extraordinary prospects for the field.

Experience around Odendaalsrus exemplified the chance elements in mineral exploration. The Geduld hole had been drilled on the boundary between the farms Geduld and Friedsheim within less than a mile of the options surrendered by the Corner House. From boreholes in the Geduld area was to come the famous Free State Geduld mine, one of the world's richest. However there were compensations of a kind for Corner House from the knowledge that the decisions to drop options to the north of Odendaalsrus had been proved sound. They were taken up by JCI which floated Freddies North and Freddies South Mines, struggling and unprofitable ventures, even when consolidated. The options held by Corner House to the east proved valueless.

At the end of 1945 Sir Clive Baillieu (later Lord Baillieu), formerly Deputy Chairman of Dunlops, had become Chairman of Central Mining in London. A big man physically, he had a wide knowledge of international business, and a genuine entrepreneurial spirit, well-suited to mining. He visited Johannesburg for the first time in 1946 and delighted Corner House personnel by declaring:

> Neither the Corner House, nor the group, nor the country, nor the industry, was built upon the lines of safety first. It called for great courage with, of course, the right admixture of luck and great administrative capacity ... I am convinced that opportunity for the display of the same native qualities of courage and resource still knocks at the door of those who have ears to listen ...
>
> We know there are no safe bets in mining, but we also know that the prizes are great for those who have the courage and the resources to persist.

Martin died in 1948 and was succeeded by W.H.A. Lawrence, a man of brilliant intellect. He had born the brunt of affairs during Martin's war-time absences on Government business, and his retiring nature had been accentuated by the trials and pressures of those years. Among his chief lieutenants, eager for new ventures, were Gordon V. Richdale, Brigadier Ralph Stokes and Pinkie Hill. To them would fall the principal roles in pulling the group's Free State chestnuts out of the fire. Richdale had come from the Bank of England in 1939 and, showing a quick grasp of mining affairs, had risen rapidly to a key executive position in the Corner House. Stokes, after his distinguished war service (he was 60 when war broke out), had been made a director of Central Mining in London and sent to Johannesburg as Technical Director with a military-type directive: 'Get us a mine in the Free State'. Having largely lost out in the Central Free State, Richdale and Stokes, like other mining entrepreneurs, focussed their attention further south. A borehole sunk towards the end of 1948 on the farm Harmonie revealed a high gold value at a depth of 1 200 metres. Richdale has recorded in his autobiography *The Sunlit Years* that this borehole when taken together with the results of other drillings, indicated that 'Harmonie might be one of the plums of the whole field'. Anglo Transvaal Consolidated, later to launch the Virginia and Merriespruit mines in the same area in concert with the Kennecott Mining Company of the United States, had its eyes on Harmonie. Unhappily for that mining house it did not enjoy good relations with a key figure, Norbert Erleigh.

Erleigh, a popular and prominent personality in social and sporting circles, and Joseph Milne, a Jewish financier of Lithuanian origin, were the principal shareholders in Union Free State Coal and Gold Mines which held control of the Harmonie area. They were anxious to sell, but the situation was complicated by the fact that they were both being prosecuted for alleged contraventions of the Companies Act. Their books were undergoing police examination, and their business was in a state of suspended animation.

Stokes was sitting in his office in the Corner House one day when Richdale walked in and said: 'Does the Board really want a Free State mine? There's a man in my office who wants to sell us one'. The man was Norbert Erleigh. He had also tried to sell Harmonie to Gold Fields. Like Rand Mines, Gold Fields' head office was in London in those days, and its board there drew back from dealing with the already-notorious Milne and Erleigh. Richdale however perceived the advantages that would accrue from taking control of the vital area, and decided to see what he could do.

> It was a case of fishing in muddy waters, and I decided to see whether I could land a really big catch. I would step in where more experienced people hesitated to tread. I therefore invited Milne and Erleigh to come and see me and I opened negotiations with them.

For several weeks there were almost daily discussions. Then Richdale and Hill flew to London to explain to the Board the technical nature of the project, and the likely yield on the substantial investment required. Baillieu gave his support and the Board agreed to authorize the expenditure of R4 m.

Richdale and Hill returned and negotiated the purchase of control for R3,3 m. Four more boreholes were then sunk and a year later the new gold mine came into being with Richdale as its chairman. Hill was appointed its consulting engineer and charged with bringing it into operation. The mine's name was anglicized as Harmony. It would cost

R1,9 m before Richdale and Hill were absolutely certain that they had really got a rich gold mine, and it would cost R50 m to bring the mine to full production, huge sums for those times.

The deal had one dreadful result for Corner House which regarded its good reputation, guarded across more than 50 years, as a principal asset. Milne and Erleigh sought also to sell to the Corner House their rights on the farm Erfdeel with its promise of another profitable gold mine to the north of Harmony. Negotiations were opened and at one time the only stumbling block was the high price demanded. In a routine manner Rand Mines Laboratories assayed the cores from Milne's drilling operations on Erfdeel, it being common practice for mining houses with the facilities to carry out assays to do so for companies lacking them.

Hill remembers

> On arriving at Corner House one afternoon I found our Chief Consulting Geologist, Dr Rodney Bridges, in an excited state. He said 'fantastic values have been found in the Erfdeel borehole'. I asked him what he meant by fantastic — the answer shook me, and because the core had not shown visible gold I expressed my concern.

The assay certificate showed a result giving more than double the value of the fabulous Geduld 1 borehole. Piet Meiring, the journalist and writer, then on *Die Transvaler*, recorded that he was awakened in the night by a telephone call from Milne who said: 'I just want to tell you that we have struck the biggest gold find of all time on Erfdeel'. Publication sparked the inevitable boom in Erfdeel shares, with dramatic profit-taking followed by huge losses as the facts emerged.

Corner House put in hand an immediate investigation. Hill went to the laboratory:

> There was some residue from the crushed core and when tested for its gold content it was patently clear that the published results were those of a 'salted' sample. To check the matter further the borehole was diverted to cut the reef a few inches away from the original intersection, the sample from the core assayed only about 250 inch-dwts, and our suspicion of the salting was confirmed.

Richdale commented in *The Sunlit Years*: 'This was salting in its crudest and most unsubtle form, and I can only suppose that the salter's hand was shaking so much that he wildly overplayed the part he was paid to perform.'

Joseph Milne and a laboratory assayer were brought to trial. Milne was found not guilty. The assayer was convicted and sentenced to a term of imprisonment. Milne and Erleigh were brought to the trial pending for contraventions of the Companies Act and received stiff prison sentences on that score.

The night before Erleigh went to jail there was a ball in Johannesburg, and Erleigh was there in white tie and tails, dancing away quite cheerfully, greeting everybody: 'See you when I come out'. Then off he went for five years in jail where he is said to have proved a trial to the warders.

Although Hill was not the senior consulting engineer at the Corner House he was made solely responsible for the planning and development of Harmony from grass roots. He flew down there with Richdale in the company aircraft to negotiate the purchase of the 405 hectares of farmland on which to build the surface plant and offices, and the accommodation for employees. Buster Fowler was appointed Acting Manager at the start.

The site of what was to become one of the great mines of the world was located in desolate farmland approached by rough farm tracks, with only an occasional farmstead to break the illusion of wilderness. From a mining viewpoint this was no illusion, for Harmony was an infrastructural wilderness: every facility needed would have to be specially provided. As elsewhere in the new field, roads, railways, powerlines, hospital services, recreational and sporting facilities would all have to be constructed, and water would have to be piped 80 kms from the Vaal by the Rand Water Board.

Syd Newman, later Chairman of Lonhro in South Africa, went there in the early days as planning manager. He, his wife and their children lived in the old Harmonie farmhouse.

> At Harmony there was nothing, not even a single store. We only owned one car and I needed that for work. This meant one's poor wife had to drive 15 miles on Saturdays to get provisions for the week and what you forgot you did without. Then every few weeks or so before the Spring rains the dust storms would come. I remember sitting in my office and being unable to see the mine headgear a hundred yards away. The dust blotted out all visibility, and afterwards covered everything like a carpet, ...

Bob Plewman was there as assistant manager:

> You know what? Farmers got more compensation for ploughed land than pasture so they ploughed everything in sight. The result was the dust. I flew down in a company plane and there was dust up to 6 000 feet. I have been on the ground at Harmony in a dust storm when the

traffic had to stop. One just could not drive. Cars pulled into the side of the road and waited for the dust to clear. It was pitch dark. The headlights were just reflected back — a genuine Sahara-type dust storm. In time the grass grew and was the biggest contributor to getting rid of the dust – though we also imported dust from other parts of the Free State.

Sinking of the ventilation shaft and the first of the main hoisting shafts began at Harmony in August 1950. Some of the ground was 'bad' and water was encountered at certain depths, requiring to be sealed off by cementation. A photograph of those days shows the diminutive Hill in a shaft sinkers' bucket or kibble being lowered underground. Sharing the bucket with him are the tall, burly figures of Lord Baillieu, Gordon Richdale, and other sturdy mining men. Buster Fowler says that when he saw Hill peering over the edge of the bucket, dwarfed by his companions, he told him 'You should have taken a box to stand on'. He swears that Hill replied: 'But I am standing on a box.'

In July 1952 the shaft intersected the Basal Reef, the main gold-bearing horizon in the Orange Free State. Richdale went down.

> It was very exciting examining the gold-bearing rock in situ. We had spent several million pounds already and yet this was the first time anyone had seen the reef... It contained excellent values. We also found that the Basal Reef contained uranium, a *bonsella* we had not counted on when we bought the property.

Another who would visit Harmony was Charles Engelhard Junior, son of the proprietor of the American firm of Baker, one of the world's big dealers in precious metals. Young

Charles, who had served as an instructor in US bombers and fighters during the war, was soon to succeed his father and expand the Engelhard empire internationally. He would play a prominent part in South African mining, and would entertain handsomely at The Court House, the fabulous mansion in Hyde Park, Johannesburg. A colourful personality, Engelhard was a short, stocky man, who became a short, stout man with heavy jowls, latterly addicted to Coca Cola.

In later years Hill took Engelhard to play golf at Royal Johannesburg, a traditional establishment with a firm attachment to the rules of decorum circumscribing what an English (or South African) gentleman might wear on its golf courses. Newman recalls:

> Most golf courses were reasonably strict in those days and Royal Johannesburg has always been especially so. So help me! Engelhard walks out of the changeroom in a brightly coloured Hawaiian shirt, Bermuda shorts below his knees, little short socks, and takkies. The club secretary was an absolute stickler about dress, etiquette and so on. There was no way Engelhard would have been allowed out on the course, he would have been out the gate in two minutes.

Hill had to use all his persuasive skills on the club secretary, begging special dispensation just once for a distinguished American visitor who had taken huge interests in South African mines; and he added for good measure: 'If you upset him he'll probably buy the club and fire you'.

Shaft sinking went ahead with great celerity. Hill, ever innovative, tried a new way of shaft sinking, providing for simultaneous sinking and lining. This was not an experiment that proved generally applicable but it produced fast sinking at Harmony, resulting in minor embarrassment for Corner House because cash expenditure ran ahead of forecasts. As development proceeded world tunnelling records were broken. Holing through on the main haulage between the two shafts was achieved in November 1953.

Plewman regards Harmony as

> the mine that Pinkie built. Still a most extraordinary mine. Pinkie had changed the face of Durban Deep and made it a place that people could live happily in and feel they belonged to. He followed this course from the start at Harmony. He employed the well-known landscape artist Joane Pim, as other mines would later. It was one of the features that made Harmony what it was.

Hill fully backed Joane Pim in a concept that took advantage of the undulating surface of Harmony. Management found that it was no use bucking the forceful lady. When they complained to head office about her sweeping plans for landscaping and tree planting, the word would come back from Hill: 'We just ought to do what Joane Pim says'.

The plans for Harmony included, naturally, a golf course. Newman recalls that Hill's regular visits to Harmony included a round of golf.

> He was crazy on golf. As soon as we had finished our discussions we'd go round the course like rabbits until it was time for him to catch his plane back to Johannesburg at 3 p.m.

In his desire to keep the surface of Harmony clean and attractive Hill was ably assisted by Roy Bryant who was appointed the first permanent manager. Bryant, like Richdale, would in later years be picked out by Engelhard to play a key role in the Engelhard industrial empire in the United States. He is remembered as a mine manager with a passion for detail — and for tidy 'housekeeping'. He used to write notes, using green ink on pink paper, up to ten o'clock at night, drawing the attention of subordinates to points of detail. The notes would be numbered, registered — and followed up. Bald-headed Bryant was known on the mine as 'Curly'.

He wrote quite a number of notes to D.A. Cochrane, the famous master sinker, complaining that the Black shaft sinkers were cleaning the kibbles by beating them with seven-pound hammers, instead of hosing them out — eventually damaging the kibbles. Cochrane got hold of a big piece of steel plate and had it beaten in the middle of the night shift. Boom, boom, boom ... rang the chimes across the sleeping mine. Cochrane watched the lights come on in Bryant's house over on the hill and Bryant come out on the veranda in his pyjamas. In the morning he was down at the shaft: 'Cochrane, they're beating the kibbles again'. 'No, Mr Bryant, come and have a look' ...

Then there was the observant banksman, Jordaan, who recounted:

> Old Curly comes down to the shaft with his Packard and gets out and he looks and goes away. A little later old Sutton, the Resident Engineer, comes down and then he goes away. Not long after comes Post Toasties (Poustie), the Section Engineer. Then the foreman carpenter comes down, he gets out and picks up three six-inch nails and puts them in the van, and off he goes. About an hour later Curly says to me: 'Have they picked up those nails yet?'

Apart from ensuring that Harmony would set a new style and standard in the layout of its surface, Hill sought to procure for its Black workers the best possible, and battled successfully with the Government and the municpality to obtain authority to build a village of houses for married Black workers on the permanent staff. For supervisory employees he built houses of a style and standard that caused raised eyebrows and some back-biting at head office. There were still those around who thought that mine officials should live in drab terrace homes. But the growing attraction of Harmony as a place to live and work enabled Hill to attract to the mine an unusually high number of graduate engineers. Overall, Corner House deployed a dazzling array of talent in the Harmony project. At one time there were five Rhodes Scholars among them: Hill, and R.E.M. Blakeway, an executive director, and on the mine, Newman, Plewman and Dr J.F.K. Cooke, who managed the uranium plant. Employees were encouraged to come forward with ideas and suggestions. Many of the innovative ideas adopted by the industry at that time came out of Harmony.

Harmony began production on 11 September, 1954. The following year it showed a profit of R2 517 328 from gold and half as much again from uranium. There was never much doubt thereafter that Harmony would be a highly profitable venture, and if there was ever a question raised against expenditure called for to expand the mine, Hill was ready to plead its necessity with eloquence.

In the event Harmony did expand and grasp the opportunities that came its way. And due to unpredictable events, it was to become one of the first of the super mines that today are a feature of the mining scene. In 1956, nearby Merriespruit, the mine developed by Anglo Vaal with high hopes, and powerfully backed by American capital, was flooded by a huge inrush of underground water, causing tragic loss of life and the drowning of the mine.

Nothing highlights more vividly the element of chance in mining than the flooding of Merriespruit, for at about the same time Harmony might so easily have suffered the same grim fate. Edwin W. Thiel, who had succeeded Bryant as Harmony's manager, was telephoned one morning with the news that water had burst through into the workings. The first inrush amounted to seven million litres, and the volume of floodwater rapidly increased.

> We had only just completed our pumping installation two weeks before. As the inflow increased the pumping capacity was there to match it. But if the flood had come a fortnight earlier we wouldn't have been able to handle the volume and if you can't handle such a huge inrush it will completely flood the workings.
> I went down underground at once and well remember wading waist deep in water at the lowest level because someone had blocked the water from going down to the pump station... I got them to blast down a wall... .

Harmony was able to handle without fuss, within its own resources, a near-disaster. The tragic flooding of neighbouring Merriespruit would require the spending of huge sums, and barren years, while pumping dry the flooded shafts and galleries.

The fortunes of Harmony, Merriespruit and Anglo Vaal's neighbouring Virginia mine, became increasingly interwoven as it was appreciated that their full potential in both gold and uranium could best be realised by interdependence and co-operation. As part of this process, Hill engineered the management of Harmony and Merriespruit as a single operation. The culmination was the incorporation into Harmony in 1973 of Merriespruit and Virginia as a single super mine administered by the Corner House.

In 1988 that mine complex produced 27 343 kilograms of gold and 158 900 kilograms of uranium at a profit of more than R77 million. But the minds of those who were involved at the start of the mine would never forget the spirit of the early years, and the fun born of good companionship in hard times. Harmony had its first big social function on 17 January 1950. Richdale and his wife Mary flew down with the Pinkie Hills and the Buster Fowlers, all splendid party people. They danced to the music of a local band in a room which was too small and had a concrete floor covered with mealie flour to help the dancers' feet glide. They were soon dancing in a choking cloud of mealie dust.

> The heat was unbearable, but no one minded, and we all danced furiously ... It was certainly an evening which none of us will ever forget.

Those pioneer days passed, and Virginia became a thriving township superimposed on its underground counterpart, where thousands worked in its deep places, reached along a system of haulage ways and tunnels, totalling many hundreds of kilometres in length; and returned at the shift-end to pleasant places to live with gardens, green lawns, trees and parks, and the amenities of civilization. Seeing the progress made and marvelling, Richdale harks back to the days when

> It was barren and bleak and hot and dusty, a vast silent expanse of nothing, with Buster and Pinkie and me sitting under a rock eating sandwiches out of a paper bag and drinking beer out of the bottle. And I think 'those were the days'. And don't let anyone tell you that there is no romance in mining. There's more real romance in mining than in a whole library of love stories.

CHAPTER SEVEN

Alarms and Excursions

Transfer to head office in Johannesburg for a mine manager is a traumatic experience not wholly cushioned by the pleasures of promotion and the attainment of the status of consulting engineer.

On the mine the manager is not just king-pin, he is king. At head office he is one of a striving, illustrious team. On the mine nothing is done without his nod: no important social or recreational activity launched without his patronage. His home is luxurious, and wholly maintained by willing artisans on the engineering staff. In Johannesburg he must find a house, and cope with the business of running it, and its financing, with assistance no doubt, but without the umbrella of the mine. More than one consulting engineer has reflected that life in the lonely eminence of head office, at times with only a secretary to chat to, was a poor exchange for total involvement in the life of a mine, and its surrounding district. But at head office there are new, tough problems, and these men are chosen because it is in their nature to grasp challenge readily.

Under arrangements then customary at Corner House the consultants in Johannesburg were appointed by Central Mining in London, and were on the staff of that corporation, while acting as advisers to the group's mines in South Africa, and to Rand Mines which administered them.

On 26 April, 1947, Hill wrote to Baillieu:

I have been in harness for just over a fortnight and settling down to my new responsibilities is proceeding smoothly. There are of course still lingering longings for Durban Deep ... in regard to which I still cherish the secret ambition that it will be second to none on the Witwatersrand in terms of appearance, its spirit of co-operation and friendliness, and its general overall efficiency.

Next on my list is the New Modder ... its life is very short, and the battle will be to keep it going. Then there is Welgedacht, where the challenge seems to be 'Make a mine of me if you can'. Needless to say the challenge is being met ... and I think Smuts* will do well. Last but not least, I have been given the TGME (Transvaal Gold Mining Estates at Pilgrim's Rest) and Glynn's Lydenburg. So I shall have a producing mine, a dying mine, a mine trying to be born, and two mines 'out in the blue'. In addition to the mines, however, investigations will be under my care. I am very pleased about this ... .

May I make use of your generous offer to send me literature on developments in the field of management?

'Investigations' meant that Hill was in charge of the search for mineral deposits on which new mines could be developed to replace the old mines nearing the end of their working lives. This was to prove the most important part of his brief, leading to Harmony gold mine, and to the abortive — and abrasive — negotiations with Joseph Milne over Erfdeel. It also brought frustration when his enthusiasm for new ventures did not win the support of the Board in Johannesburg, or if, when they did, they failed to clear the hurdle of a lingering conservatism in London. But

---

* Japie Smuts, destined to die in harness at an early age, was the son of Field Marshall, Smuts, then Prime Minister

if he had to endure a measure of frustration he also knew how to relax. Newman remembers:

> Pinkie claimed that when he went to head office, his doctor told him 'You've been a mine manager and you're very busy and active. You mustn't get inactive. You must take exercise. You should play a lot of golf!' So he decided to play every Thursday afternoon. Never mind what the Chairman said, nor what anyone else said, every Thursday Pinkie went to golf. Throughout his life he never missed, and it was quite a joke among us that if we had a meeting on Thursday morning, round about 11 o'clock this sort of haze would come into his eyes. Afterwards it was useless going on. He wasn't listening, and he'd say, 'Well that's all for today'. He'd go and play golf. We realised that after eleven on Thursdays we might as well close the agenda.

Also there to help him relax was the background of the home that Dora ran in Johannesburg, and the family they raised there. David had been born in December 1936, and proved to be retarded. Margaret followed in 1938. Robert Oliver was born at the time of the move to ERPM in 1939 and Penny in 1943.

The Hill's lived first at White Gables, in Anerley Road, Parktown, remembered in the family for Hill's battle with burglars.

> My father-in-law, Sir Robert Kotzé, was staying with us. At about 2 o'clock in the morning we heard him shouting. I ran through the passage and into the dining room where I saw a light. There was a man sitting on the floor packing up our silver. Another man was collecting more. Without thinking I sprang onto the man on the

floor and found myself locked in a life-and-death struggle during which two of my fingernails were ripped off.

Meanwhile Dora had freed her father who had been locked in his bedroom, and the two then rushed in to my aid. The second robber who was about to tackle me as well, took fright and jumped out the window. But when he saw it was just a woman and an old man he started to climb back in again ... I heard a banging noise and looked up from my struggle to see Dora beating him about the head with a heavy silver tray. Then the big man I was struggling with broke loose and jumped out of the window ... He left a dagger lying on the floor. If he had been given a chance to grasp it it would have been the end of me.

There was an amusing finale to what could have been a tragedy.

We telephoned the police and a van arrived with two White policemen, two Black policemen and a Black suspect, arrested for another offence. The two White policemen came into the house. Then we heard the van's hooter sounding. We rushed outside to find the suspect had escaped, and was running down the road pursued by the two Black policemen. We all joined in ... the suspect, followed by two Black policemen, two White policemen and me, all running down the road. Soon my slippers fell off and Dora joined the cavalcade, running after me, shouting 'Sweetie, your slippers!'

In June 1951 Dora went to view a house on sale in The Valley Road. She saw a double-storey, stone and stucco-faced mansion on two acres with a glorious view across the

The Terraces – The Hill family home at Kroonstad. The gardens ran down to the Valsch River.

The four young brothers Hill: Pinkie, Sonnie, David and Denston. All scrum-halves in embryo. David played against the All Blacks and Pinkie for Wits.

The Rhodes Scholar. New College, Oxford.

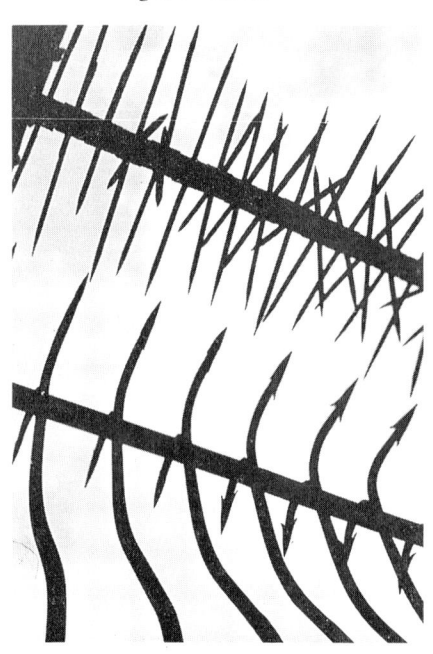

The captions to these pictures in Hill's Oxford album read 'Can be scaled!' and 'Despite these'.

Delegates to an international students' congress on the steps of Budapest palace. Hill represented the National Union of South African Students (NUSAS).

Hill and Leif Egeland, pilot officers of the University Air Squadron (RAF). Egeland would later become High Commissioner in London.

Hill (centre) and other young pilots await the call at RAF Manston, a scene evocative of the airfield's role in the Battle of Britain, a decade later.

The brilliant J.H. Hofmeyr, who was appointed the first principal of the University of the Witwatersrand at the age of 27.

Sir Robert Kotzé. Sketch from *The Reef* shows him with the instrument he invented for measuring the dust in mine air.

Hill and Dora Kotzé after their marriage. They celebrated their Golden Wedding in 1986.

The Bell House. Aerial view of the Hill home in The Valley Road, Parktown, Johannesburg.

Sketch of Hill.

Going under at ERPM – Charles Engelhard in white miners' hat, and (right), Peter Anderson, Engelhard's successor as Chairman of Rand Mines.

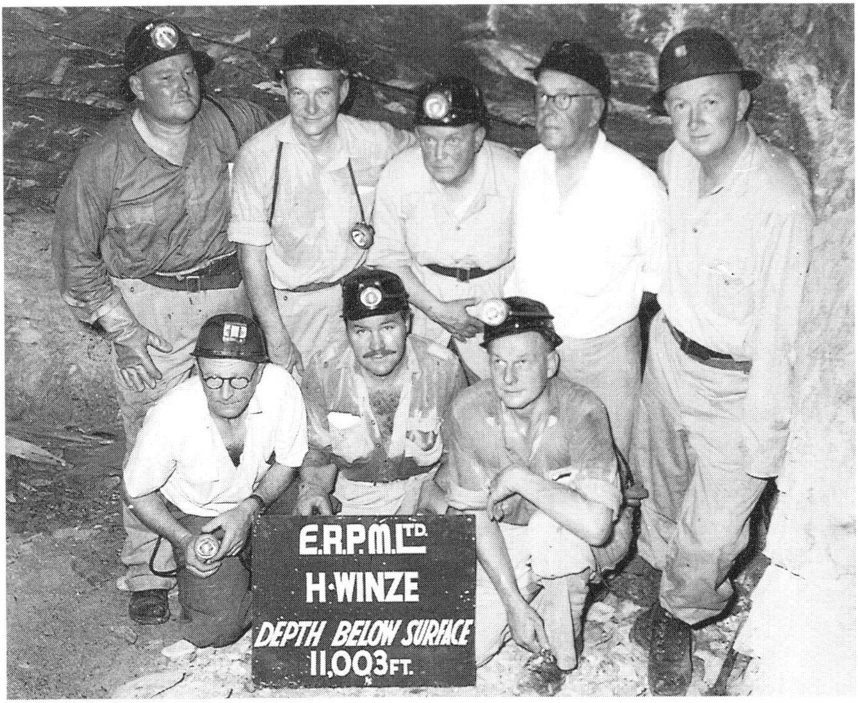

Deepest men on earth: celebrating ERPM's achievement of world record depth. A.R.C. 'Buster' Fowler, a consulting engineer is on the right.

The Long and the Short and the Tall go down the first sinking shaft at Harmony gold mine. Hill is dwarfed by Gordon Richdale, S.R. Bryant, Lord Baillieu (behind Hill), a shaft sinker, The Hon Edward Baillieu (Lord Baillieu's son) and D. Cochrane, Master Sinker.

Lord Baillieu.

Charles Engelhard.

Harmony at grass roots.

Mrs W.H. Lawrence, wife of the then Chairman of Rand Mines, pours the first gold bar at Harmony.

The Corner House, headquarters of Rand Mines in Johannesburg.

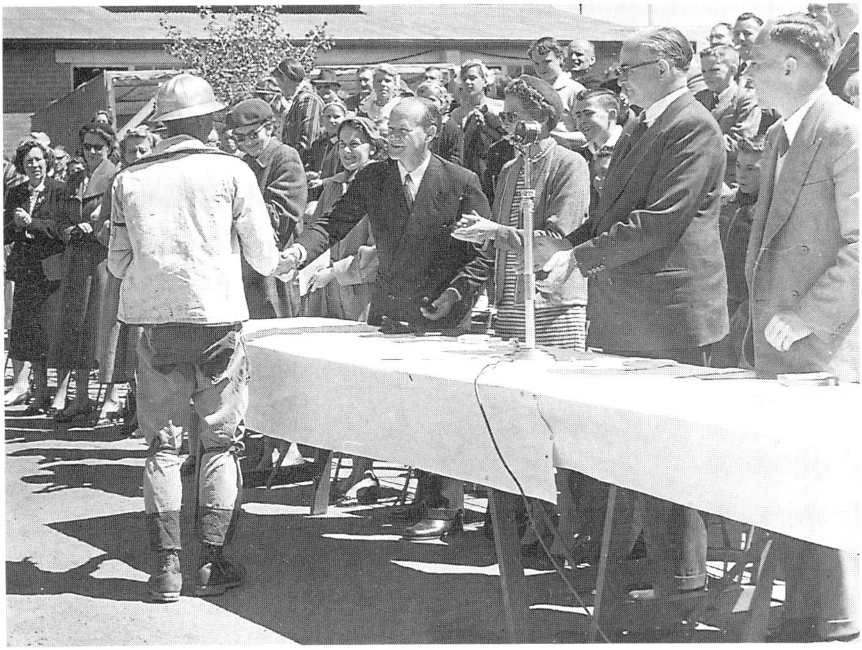

Mine safety function – honouring a brave man.

The Council for Scientific and Industrial Research in session. Hill was appointed in 1954 and served for 17 years.

Receiving the honorary degree of Doctor of Philosophy from Prof E.J. Marais, Principal and Vice-Chancellor, Port Elizabeth University.

Mrs Dora Hill christening Rand Mines aircraft.

Golf, a lifelong passion. Syd Newman is on the right.

Hill and Professor Isabel White, founders and Honorary Fellows of the Institute of Personnel Management (Southern Africa).

Honorary degree of Doctor of Laws: the capping by B.L. Bernstein, Chancellor of Wits, in 1978.

CITATION

Behind Dr F G Hill lies a career of distinction and achievement. He ranks with the most distinguished mining engineers that have ever been engaged in the South African mining industry. Amongst others, he instituted technology for shaft pillar extraction; studied high rock stress in gold mines; was instrumental in introducing personnel departments on mines; and played a leading role in the establishment of the University of the Witwatersrand Business School.

Dr Hill also had a special interest in the problem of dust control and pneumoconiosis. His interest and role was exemplified by the fact that he was Chairman of the Government's Pneumoconiosis Research Unit, delivered a number of papers and contributions on the subject and he was responsible for the establishment of the Corner House Laboratories at Richmond for addressing the problems of ventilation and dust control.

With fellow pioneer, Dr William Bleloch, he persuaded Rand Mines to institute the development of a ferrochrome industry, thereby preparing the way for the production of stainless steel in the country. His more than 100 scientific papers deal mainly with rockbursts and strata control in deep mines, ventilation in mines, mining methods, dust control and prevention of pneumoconiosis, personnel management, deep level mining practice and the exploitation of ultra-deep gold deposits.

For his manifold outstanding contributions, many honours have been conferred on Dr Hill, not only in South Africa but also overseas. Mining and Metallurgical Societies awarded him for various contributions, no less than three gold medals. In addition the South African Institute of Mining and Metallurgy honoured him in 1982 with their premier award, The Brigadier Stokes Memorial Award, for the highest achievement and contribution by an individual in the field of mining and metallurgy in South Africa.

For exceptional merit by rendering exceptionally meritorious service in the general public interest, The Order for Meritorious Service, Gold, is awarded to Dr Francis George Hill.

Citation for The Order for Meritorious Service (Gold), awarded in 1989.

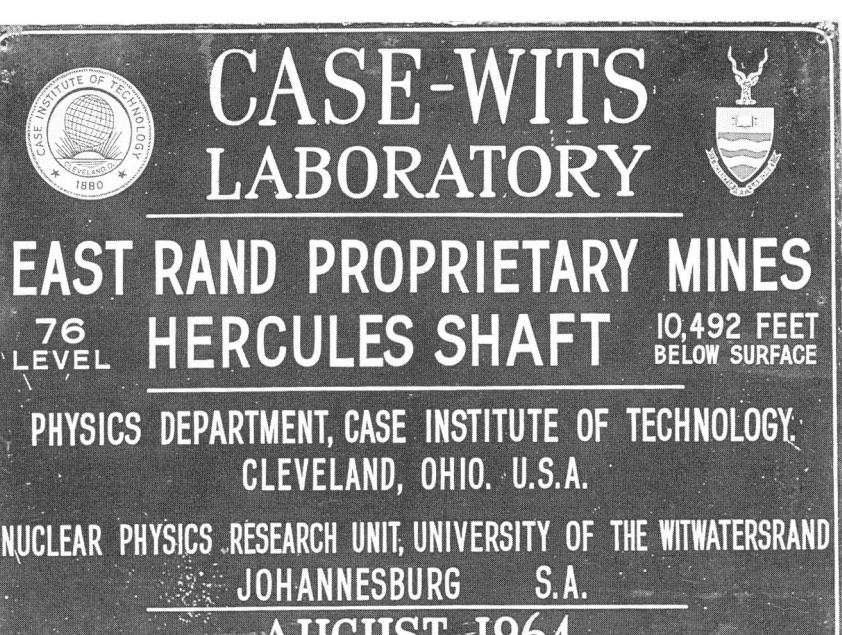

The sign at the entrance to the original laboratory established by Wits and the Case Institute of Technology, Cleveland, Ohio on 76 level of ERPM.

Neutrino detector 10 492 feet underground used to prove in nature the existence of the subnuclear particle known as a neutrino.

The Standard Bank Centre, opened in August 1990, is built on top of the main gold-bearing conglomerate of the Rand gold field. It covers what was once the site of shafts, and the manager's house at the Ferreira mine.

The stope of the Ferreira gold mine preserved three levels below ground at the Standard Bank Centre in Simmonds Street, Johannesburg illustrates the link between modern Johannesburg and its mining past. Hill's investigations revealed that shallowly-undermined ground would gradually settle and become safe for building.

northern suburbs. It had been built for a director of African Explosives in the spacious style then fashionable in Parktown, with high ceilings, an imposing entrance hall and stairway, much splendid wood pannelling. Dora recalls that as she walked into that entrance hall she was surprised by the sudden thought: 'Oh, but this is my house!' Hill did not want to move, and demurred at first, but Dora had her way and it was bought for R33 000. They have lived in it ever since. There Pinkie and Dora entertained in their special way their friends, and a succession of visitors from overseas. The homely ambience it acquired means much to them, and they are deeply attached to its caringly-tended gardens, its trees grown tall and its ivy-covered walls.

At head office Hill continued to promote the expansion of personnel management, arranging for Reinald Hofmeyr to study overseas in 1948 and bringing him into Johannesburg in 1955 as Group Personnel Manager charged with developing personnel departments throughout the group. The growth of this work brought Hill into association with Dr Simon Biesheuvel who had distinguished himself during the war as head of the aptitude testing branch of the South African Air Force, and was now the Director of the National Institute for Personnel Research (NIPR) of the Council for Industrial and Scientific Research (CSIR).

Union Corporation under T.P. Stratten, like Hill a Rhodes Scholar, had taken a lead in entrusting Biesheuvel with the evolution of a scientifically-based system of simple tests to evaluate the abilities and manual skills of Black workers. It was an approach which won the ready support of Corner House. Hill appointed Frits Boer to take charge of testing and set it up for all Corner House mines.

The migrant labourers on which the industry relied came from the tribal areas of South Africa, and the then British High Commission Territories of Basutoland (now independent Lesotho), Bechuanaland (Botswana) and Swaziland; and from countries beyond, principally Mozambique with its long tradition of mining work at Kimberley and on the Reef. These men, largely illiterate, could be employed on simple pick-and-shovel work in stopes, drives or shafts, on 'tramming' ore along the haulage ways, or on more sophisticated labour such as the operation of pneumatic drills, or winch driving. A proportion, after experience, would be appointed boss boys or team leaders, to assist White supervisors in the chain of command. Allocation of new recruits to job categories was largely a matter for personal judgement by the official concerned, sometimes arrived at 'by guess or by God', coloured by the prevalent belief that certain tribes were best suited to particular types of work. Thus, it was generally accepted that Basutos had a special aptitude for the hard, and relatively hazardous, manual labour of shaft sinking, while Shangaans from Mozambique seemed to show a special aptitude for work of a mechanical nature. This belief in tribal aptitudes evoked a reciprocal tendency for tribes to regard certain work as their own.

A stumbling block in the way of aptitude testing was the multiplicity of languages found among entrants, and the problem of communicating with them ahead of the usual course of instruction in the mines' lingua franca, *fanakalo*. This problem was resolved by the use of silent film to explain by demonstration what was required before each of the series of tests. Biesheuvel says that the aptitude tests then developed by the NIPR have stood the test of time remarkably well. An examination more than 30 years later showed that the satisfactory correlation between test and job performance had changed little over the years. Aptitude testing, followed by a period in the training school on the indicated job, became part of the mining scene.

Once the NIPR had shown in a realistic way what it could achieve in putting round pegs into round holes, the doors of the mining industry opened ever-wider to it. It was soon conducting surveys on the attitude of Black employees to varying aspects of work and life on the mines.

Hofmeyr recalls that one of the NIPR's early projects for Hill at Corner House concerned the bonus system and the boss boy's understanding of it.

> Group production bonuses were very much in vogue and a story I've always treasured related to a boss boy, or team leader as we would call him today, who was asked whether he and his colleagues knew how their bonuses were calculated. He replied: 'No! Sometimes we get a big bonus, and sometimes we get a small bonus; it's all part of the White man's madness'.

Another survey concerned the relevant popularity of individual mines. It was found that contrary to expectation the most important factor in the mind of the Black worker was neither pay (though this ranked high), nor the discomfort and dangers of work underground, but human relationships, the manner of his treatment underground and in the hostels, and the interest shown by management in his well-being.

The survey report commented:

> ... it often happens that a mine's unpopularity ... is attributed to its underground mining conditions. These are unalterable, and the conclusion reached is that nothing can be done, and no further effort need be made. This is not the case. Natives are prepared to tolerate difficult underground conditions, provided working conditions are bearable, and treatment is just, sympathetic and comprehended by them.

The NIPR pioneered the employment of Black psychologists who could talk to Black mineworkers in their own language; and ascertain what they really thought about conditions. Information of this kind had a major influence on the improvements introduced in the planning of new mines, or in the modification of the old.

Biesheuvel remembers that it was not easy at first to convince the mining industry of the benefit of the work the Institute was doing:

> We could not have succeeded without the support of men like Stratten and Hill. It was easy to go off the deep end because I was of course concerned for my staff who were having a difficult time on the mines. Maybe I overreacted a bit. Pinkie would say to me 'You know you were a bit too aggressive'. I learnt one or two lessons in that way.
>
> Pinkie had the personality make-up which produced co-operation rather than confrontation. The structure of the industry was almost military in its rigidity and contained a wide spectrum of jobs. He was able to cut across hard and fast ideas and overcome resistance. He did an enormous job for the mines by making them more conscious of the need to motivate people properly. This spread so that he made a major contribution to industry generally. Industry often took its example from the mines.

Further advantage for the mining industry flowed from Hill's personal flair in recognising ability, from the encouragement he gave to able young men, and the interest he maintained in their careers.

David Ortlepp, head of the Rock Mechanics Department of Anglo American's Gold Division, recalls that he owed to

Hill an essential foundation to the career that has made him a world authority on combating rockbursts.

> I graduated from Wits in 1952 with the Chamber of Mines scholarship and gold medal which then required that the incumbent should travel. I wanted to study at a research institute rather than just travel. I was very young — perhaps more comfortable at the thought of going abroad and settling at a university for a couple of years. I had intended to approach Anglo for appointment as a graduate learner. I found they were totally unsympathetic to the idea that I should break service and go abroad for a time. The attitude was: 'Well, when you come back we will consider employing you'. The Chamber of Mines was quite unsympathetic as well to my going abroad for post-graduate study at a research institute rather than travel. So somewhat depressed at these two manifestations of lack of encouragement I was wandering along Simmonds Street near the Corner House when I bumped into a contemporary of mine at Wits University. He had joined the Corner House. When I poured out my tale of woe he said 'Come upstairs right now'.
>
> I was introduced to Alistair Black who was Hill's technical assistant at the time, who said: 'That's absolute nonsense. If you want to go to university overseas we can help the Chamber of Mines to see it in that light. A word with Pinkie Hill, or through him to the Chamber, and I am sure it will happen.'

It did happen. Ortlepp joined Corner House where he would stay for many years. He spent from mid-1955 to mid-1957 studying the infant science of rock mechanics at a famous mining institution, McGill University in Canada.

He returned to spend eight years working closely with Mischi Barcza, Hill's right-hand man on research, followed by eight years studying rock mechanics under front-line mining conditions at ERPM.

Plewman comments:

> It is really quite an interesting thing that when Alistair Black moved from the Corner House to be head of the Royal School of Mines in England there were people who had worked under Hill heading the three major mining schools — Black at the Royal, Ralph Gorges at Britain's Camborne School of Mines, and myself at Wits Department of Mining.

Newman was another who benefitted by Hill's personal interest. He had become in 1940 the second mining engineer to win a Rhodes Scholarship. But instead of going to Oxford he joined up, and served in The SA Engineering Corps and was taken prisoner-of-war. At the War's end he was impatient to begin his working life, but Hill persuaded him not to let slip the opportunity to take up his Rhodes Scholarship at Oxford. He did so attaining an MA. degree in Politics, Philosophy and Economics. He won a rugby blue, and played full-back for England.

> Hill was always alive to the chance of getting chaps into Rand Mines. While I was at Oxford he took the trouble to visit me there towards the end of my stay. I was going to spend a year travelling in the United States, but he advised me rather to come back and work. He offered me a job on Durban Deep and a house. I had just married and that clinched it.

Newman started as a 'study observer' at the beginning of

1949. The senior officials who had come up the hard way did not think much of this green university graduate.

Here was a guy, a so-called study observer, with a manager's ticket, a survey ticket, a mine captain's ticket and a blasting ticket. Well, you know, who did he think *he* was? That was the mining attitude to young graduates in those days. However, the manager was aware I was earmarked as one of Pinkie's protégés. Suddenly I moved up the scale.

I worked for a while under a mine captain who was a purist, an absolute all-perfectionist. His work was good. His planning was meticulous. Everything was as thorough as you could imagine. He worked over at No 1 Shaft which we were then establishing and he used to spend hours and hours working on his layouts to work up the Main Reef there. I remember one day Pinkie came along with the manager. Pinkie had asked to see where Newman was; it was the kind of interest he would keep up. So the manager brought Pinkie underground and the mine captain showed him the shape of his lay-outs and in which direction we were planning to go. I suppose as Consulting Engineer Pinkie felt he had to say something. So he said: 'Why are you going there? Why don't you go there?' So my boss explained all the possibilities and Pinkie said: 'Yes, I think we should change that, go there. Don't go here.'

Off they went and my boss turned back to me and he said: 'Look, he'll never come back. Leave it as it was.' So I said 'you're the boss, I work for you.'

Hill's attention was ever focused on the pursuit of excellence in management. He pioneered business executive education in the group. As early as 1948 he arranged for Buster

Fowler to attend one of the first courses run by Britain's Administrative Staff College at Henley-on-Thames. Newman and Plewman followed, and so did Edwin Thiel, Tony Petersen who became chairman of Rand Mines in later years, and other outstanding members of staff. The courses were run by a brilliant Englishman, Noel Hall, who had been an economic adviser to the British Government during the war. This became an on-going practice at the Corner House and ever since there has hardly been a senior executive who has not attended an executive training programme at an overseas business school. Initially the accent was on the course at Henley-on-Thames, but later this was broadened to include schools like the London Business School, and in the United States Harvard, Stanford and Darden, the University of Virginia.

In due course Hill set up a Co-ordination Committee and required the managers of all group mines to attend its bi-monthly meetings to discuss developments in the industry, technical advances and scientific research into mining problems. Hill was determined to write *finis* to the habit of some older managers of holding cards close to their chest. The days were ending when managers could be permitted to assert their individuality to the point of reluctance to listen to the views of others, or to accept that there were new ideas they might adapt to their mine. Hill perceived that nothing in his role was more important than co-ordination of group activities. Many of the changes that took place on the mines would flow from the seminar-type discussions of the Co-ordination Committee.

Plewman was the secretary of the committee at the outset.

It was Hill's drive that led to the committee's formation, and he was made chairman although he was not the senior consulting engineer. Changes affecting the Blacks, for example, were steered through the Co-ordination Committee. Once you had the agreement of all managers in the group, you could get what you wanted done on the mines.

If the atmosphere at Corner House grew tense at times there were always those mines 'out in the blue' at Pilgrim's Rest and Lydenburg to provide a change of scene and mental relief. Buster Fowler, by now a close friend of Hill's, became the most renowned of the remarkable men who have occupied the manager's house at Pilgrim's Rest, and a genial host to visitors. Today 'Buster's Boots' still adorn the bar in the village pub.

An official visit to Pilgrim's Rest with its shallow and open-cast mines allowed much pleasant relaxation after work and golf, and there were good parties. There was time too for rest and reflection at the manager's house. Compared to an official visit to a deep-level gold mine on the Rand it was a holiday.

On one such occasion, Hill had injured his leg, but wished to view a proposed new lay-out from a point that could only be reached by walking up a hill. Frustrated by his injury he said to Fowler: 'Well, can't you carry me up?' Fowler remarks, looking back: 'It's usual enough for consulting engineers to ride on managers' backs, but figuratively and not literally. However I got him on my back and lugged old Pinkie up to the top of the hill'.

By then gold had been mined in the lovely hills around Pilgrim's Rest for nearly 80 years. The Corner House owned another gold mine in a figurative sense in the freehold of some 80 000 acres of ground in the mist belt of the mountains which was ideally suited to afforestation. In the early years of the century tree plantings were placed under the direction of a resourceful compound manager, Robert Gardner, known as Boss Bob. Out of his imaginative and forceful activities grew the timber industry of the Transvaal. Richdale, another who relished the journeys to Pilgrim's Rest, took great interest in the plantations, and deployed his entrepreneurial expertise in extending them.

Hill delighted in the trees, and in the experiments in paper making which produced newsprint for copies of *The Star*. He had a vision of a great paper-making industry under the aegis of Corner House, but to his lasting regret the opportunity was surrendered to others. It was decided to separate the mining and forestry activities, and hand over the timber business to S.A. Forest Investments in exchange for shareholdings in that company.

Young Charles Engelhard on his first visit in 1951 had been impressed with the mining industry and the investment opportunities in South Africa. On a second visit Richdale took him to the Eastern Transvaal. Engelhard again liked what he saw. He bought a timber farm, and invested in T.G.M.E. and S.A. Forest Investments, becoming a director of both. He then offered Richdale a virtual partnership, appointment as President of all the Engelhard companies. Richdale accepted and, to Hill's regret, departed for New Jersey.

Engelhard, however, was to play a burgeoning role in South African affairs. In 1956 there were developments in the oil business in which Central Mining had long had a major interest. The Texas Company now made an offer for Trinidad Leaseholds, founded by Central Mining in 1913, and a deal was completed. While beneficial for Central Mining's shareholders, the result was a large cash surplus which in the circumstances of the Corporation invited take-over. The first to move were the Glaser brothers of Johannesburg, flush with cash from big property transactions.

Cartwright wrote in *Golden Age*:

> It created a Gilbertian situation in Johannesburg where the executives of the oldest and most highly respected mining house in South Africa were informed by the Press that they might be taken over by two gentlemen whom they knew, if they knew them at all, as successful estate agents occupying a suite of offices in a building opposite the Corner House.

Engelhard now took a hand. He sent Richdale to London where he learnt that merchant banks judged Central Mining to be dangerously vulnerable to take-over. Richdale kept Engelhard informed by cable and then, with Baillieu's approval, put the whole question of Central Mining's difficulties to Engelhard on his return. Engelhard took a typically quick, and laconic, decision: 'Let's buy'.

Engelhard and Richdale formed a consortium headed by Rothschilds and including the firms of Robert Benson, Lonsdale and Company, Charles Engelhard, Union Corporation and the International Nickel Company. In August 1957, the consortium registered a company called Rand American Investments (Proprietary) Ltd which owned virtually all the preference shares of Central Mining, as well as a large number of ordinary shares, and a substantial holding in Rand Mines. A hostile take-over had been averted.

Charles Engelhard was the first chairman, the directors including R.B. Hagart of Anglo American, Stratten of Union Corporation, C.S. Barlow, the industrialist, and Richdale. Soon after the Baron Elie de Rothschild joined the board, and so did H.F. Oppenheimer of Anglo American on the death of his father Sir Ernest.

There were to follow far-reaching changes, for the decision was taken to end Central Mining's control of its

South African mines from London and instead to grant autonomy to Rand Mines. This was a break with the tradition established in pioneer days when the Wernher Beit partnership exercised control of its South African companies through Rand Mines, most of whose directors were its paid managers, and through the consulting engineers which it appointed. Central Mining had inherited the system, once common among mining houses but now obsolete.

As Lord Baillieu put it

It has ... become apparent in recent years that there were some disadvantages in a system whereby technical and managerial services were provided by a British Company with its head office 6 000 miles away in London.

His statement must have been applauded by those at Corner House who felt that London Office, through its lack of an immediate grasp of the factors operating in South Africa, exercised a restraining hand on new enterprise.

Engelhard now became chairman of Rand Mines in a kind of non-resident capacity, making regular visits to Johannesburg from his base in the USA. His advent aroused some trepidation from the staff, which was soon dispelled by his easy manner and his determination to find new outlets for the capital and entrepreneurial skills of the company. It is said, however, that he did not share his staff's enthusiasm for morning tea, nor their veneration of the ancient brass-bound lifts in the old Corner House building on Simmonds and Commissioner Street. Plans were soon in hand for a new building a couple of hundred metres to the west, with modern offices and streamlined elevators.

Hill, having duly switched in September from employment with Central Mining, London, to employment with Rand Mines, Johannesburg, was promoted to Technical Manager, and took over leadership of the group's technical activities. In consequence ERPM once again came within his purview. The mine, rescued by the increase in the gold price following the flight from the Gold Standard in 1932, had received a further injection of new life from the sterling devaluation of 1949. As mining progressed to greater depths gold values improved, so much so that preparations were put in hand for mining at depths below 3 000 metres.

An integral part of the operation was the building of a new reduction plant, for the two existing plants were working at a cost way above the industry average. Engelhard accepted Hill's advice that an up-to-date plant, though costly, would rapidly pay for itself.

The companion project was the sinking of a sub-vertical shaft in the eastern extremity of ERPM to a depth of 2 853 metres below surface. Its purpose was dual, ventilation of the ultra-deep workings and access to the new area opened to exploration.

A crisis in the sinking of the shaft endangered the mine and produced an inspired feat of off the cuff engineering that lives vividly in Hill's memory.

> The old vertical shaft went down to 5 000 feet. We now drove a horizontal tunnel and started to sink the sub-vertical shaft to go down to 10 000 feet. The sinking team was routinely injecting cement ahead of the sinking to prevent inrushes of water from underground fissures. The diamond drills were being operated through a pipe with a stopcock on it so that any inrush of water could be turned off. At 339 feet the diamond drills struck a water-

bearing fissure. So enormous was the pressure that the water came rushing past the drill — and when the drill was withdrawn with great difficulty the pressure was so great that the stopcock could not be turned. The floodwater rose rapidly in the shaft.

We knew that if the water rose above the shaft and flooded the horizontal tunnel to the old vertical shaft from surface — well, I didn't know how the hell we would ever have got back. So it was a very dramatic situation — the water came rushing through at a tremendous rate — I can remember the chaps standing neck deep in the water, until they were more or less swimming. We then contacted the Underwater Research Group in Johannesburg and they sent out divers. In a desperate bid to stop the flow it was decided to try to get a big ring spanner onto the stopcock under water and to attach a wire rope to it, and take this up through the water to a winch in the hope that by turning the winch we could then close the stopcock. The divers went down with the big spanner. Meanwhile the water was all the time rising and shooting up at me, just a constant surge of floodwater under huge pressure. The divers couldn't see much but, operating by touch and feel, they got the spanner on, attached the wire rope, turned the winch and gradually the stopcock closed.

The biggest thrill in my life was when I saw absolute quiet on the water. The stopcock had been closed and the shaft had been saved — really one of the most dramatic experiences of my life.

With the closure of the valve, the shaft could be pumped dry and cement injected into the fissure to prevent further inrush. The way was open for ERPM to probe the ultra deeps, and it would soon reach a depth below 3 350 metres and celebrate the achievement of being the deepest mine in the world.

CHAPTER EIGHT

Pushing Back the Boundaries

By the early 1950s empirical investigation of the rockburst phenomena was well-advanced, but theoretical understanding of its mechanism had lagged. Hill perceived that there was little more that could be achieved without it. It was time to deploy the scientists.

In August 1951, he told the Chemical, Metallurgical and Mining Society that the search for improved methods of mining in areas of great pressure must be systematic — in other words there should be a new emphasis on scientific research.

> How often lately have we heard the lament that we on the Witwatersrand do insufficient research. It is true. We do far too little ... in this matter we are laggards. The problem of rock pressure cries out for more attention. It is a shocking indictment of our short-sightedness that we on the mines have not a single first-class research brain devoted continuously to this problem. The laboratories — the deep level mines are waiting. But where is the research team? Important pressure phenomena occur on our mines almost daily and give facts which if collected, arranged and debated, could build up a body of knowledge which would do much to clarify our theories and improve practice. We do not make enough use of the knowledge actually or potentially at out disposal ...

Progress cannot come this way; the approach must be more scientific; men must be put on the job who have a bent for research; they must have first-class brains and infinite patience... .

Hill had been appointed by the Government back in 1943 to a three-man committee on deep level mining, and its deliberations had stimulated support for the establishment of a national mining research institute, but nothing came of it. However, in 1945 research in South Africa received new impetus from the foundation of the Council for Scientific and Industrial Research (CSIR) on the pattern of similar bodies in Britain and elsewhere in the Commonwealth. Field Marshal Smuts, the Prime Minister, declared that the CSIR would have the dual function of conducting both pure research, and applied research that could result in great industrial advances.

In 1952 Hill took the first important step towards a scientific understanding of rockbursts by enlisting the co-operation of the CSIR in establishing an operational research team. He foresaw that out of scientific enquiry would grow new techniques, or modifications of those existing, that would reduce further the hazard of rockbursts, and death and injury among miners. The joint Corner House-CSIR team studied the physical properties of the rocks which burst, the nature of the associated stresses and strains and the effects of various mining factors and practices.

The CSIR soon appointed Hill a member of its governing council. He served for 17 years, forging valuable links between the country's leading scientists and the mining industry. In 1956 there followed appointment to the Advisory Council for Scientific Policy, later to become The Prime Minister's Advisory Council.

At the outset of the rockburst enquiry he worked closely

with two outstanding scientists, Dr A.J.A. 'Ampie' Roux, and Dr H. 'Gunter' Denkhaus. Roux would later become Director of the CSIR's National Mechanical Engineering Research Institute. Later still he would be Chairman of South Africa's Atomic Energy Board and the power behind the country's nuclear research and uranium enrichment programme. Denkhaus, who had research experience in West Germany, followed Roux as Director of the Institute, a post he held for 21 years before becoming a professor at the University of Pretoria. Denkhaus recalls:

> We three were formed by Pinkie into a committee within the framework of Rand Mines. We first of all devised a programme. Pinkie was very keen on doing statistics on rockbursts, so that their severity could be defined. We programmed mathematical analyses, tests at the laboratory into the strength of rock and, of course, underground visits. I almost qualified as a mining engineer from going underground so often.

The main outcome of this early thinking and testing by scientists was to emphasize the importance of the shape — the geometry — of mining excavations. There was solid confirmation that mining policy should be such as to avoid remnants of 'unpaying' ground left, not for support but because they were uneconomic to mine.

Denkhaus retains in the English language the accent of his German birth, and a sometimes picturesque turn of speech.

> I formalized the situation by saying that rockbursts occur wherever the geometry of the mining is funny and wherever the material of the rock is funny. On the Far East Rand the footwall consists of shale. I wouldn't say there are no rockbursts there but they are fairly rare.

They are not severe. On the Central Rand the hanging wall and the footwall are both quartzite. If the load on it increases because of local high pressure then it fails with brittle violence because there is no plastic deformation which is nature's way of relieving pressure. It is unlike shale which is ductile. When I lectured at the Institute of Mining and Metallurgy I used to take along a piece of rubber. I would show it to the audience, stretch it and release so that it shot across the room. Then I would take a piece of bubble gum, pull it and release — and nothing happened. Then I'd say 'Gentlemen, that's the difference between quartzite and shale. One is elastic, the other is plastic'. Those were the main findings of the early days. Pinkie was the driving force.

Denkhaus says that the importance of planning the geometry of mines properly was accepted by the industry. In due course this would be handled by computers which identified for the planners the areas in which great energy was locked under high pressure.

Today, too, they have rock mechanics departments on mines, and Pinkie was the initiator of that, I think you can say. When we started our enquiries, we surveyed the technical papers presented on the subject. It was apparent from these that while mine managers were good engineers their scientific background was weak — in mechanics and physics — and they had funny ideas. This has changed. Nowadays, mining students study rock mechanics as a subject. Hill, Roux and I put rock mechanics on the map. It has been further developed, you know, since those days ... But it was Hill who realised the importance of science in mining ... that science is not a matter of writing big formulae which nobody understands, but the necessary shorthand of thinking, planning. Previously, South Africa was behind other countries in the world in research — slow to start — but the fact that you are behind is no reason to sit back. You have to make your own contribution — then it becomes an exchange... you are not just a taker. Thanks to Pinkie, South Africa became the leading country internationally in the field of rock mechanics.

Hill was eleven years Denkhaus' senior, and a top man in the industry, exercising considerable power. His easy, friendly relationships with subordinates and younger men shook the German, who was used to strict formality and unaccustomed to being on first-name terms even after long association.

> He was a warm-hearted friend — not haughty. He was a big boss, but he didn't say so. It was pleasant to work with him.

The early results of the marriage between the Corner House and the CSIR brought Hill the Gold Medal of the South African Institute of Mining and Metallurgy, for the second time. Moreover the high promise of ameliorating rockbursts led the Chamber of Mines in 1956 to take over sponsorship of the programme on behalf of the industry. A Rockburst and Strata Movement Committee, representing the Chamber, the mining groups and the CSIR, was established under Hill's chairmanship. Scientists and engineers from the University of the Witwatersrand and its Bernard Price Institute of Geophysical Research were soon incorporated.

Hill was at once active in urging expansion of the research conducted by the Chamber. At that time its research organization consisted of the Biological and Chemical Research Laboratory, of which a principal feature had been work on the preservation of timber underground; a Dust and Ventilation Laboratory, concerned with the detailed examination of dust samples from mine air, and with methods of measuring and suppressing mine dust; and an Applied Physiology Laboratory. Only the last was doing research of real importance, for the work on timber preservation had, in the main, been successfully completed, while the work on dust was principally a monitoring service to the mines. The Applied Physiology Laboratory, headed by the dynamic and turbulent Professor Cyril Wyndham, had started under the CSIR, and been much encouraged by Hill who provided facilities for experiments at Corner House's City Deep. These yielded such positive results that in 1951 Hill successfully urged the Chamber to take over the laboratory. It soon established a world reputation for acclimatizing men for work in hot places, and in protecting them from heat stroke.

On 19 September, 1957, Hill sent a memorandum to the Chamber, saying that it was apparent that the Chamber's research could be expanded to the great benefit of the mines. At present many research projects were moving forward painfully slowly. They seemed to suffer from inadequate guidance and drive. The time had come for the control to be given to an overall director who would have direct access to the Gold Producers Committee, the top executive body chaired by the Chamber's president. The industry needed guidance at the highest level from a first-class research brain with the ability and the vision to assess the most rewarding lines of research. A well-thought-out and clearly-detailed programme was vitally needed. The judgement of a man experienced in assessing the calibre of research workers was essential in creating a high-quality research team.

Hill stressed that he knew of no large-scale research in industry without a director. Such an appointment at the Chamber would increase the contact with scientists outside the industry which was currently lacking. It would give the whole research effort new 'punch'.

He drew attention to the way in which the administration of the CSIR had been shaped by Dr B.J. Schonland when founding State research in 1945. There was a need to realise that research was a highly specialized function. Under the normal administrative machine, research scientists could become frustrated and their projects stultified. He quoted Sir John Russell, a noted British scientist and director of research, as saying: 'It must never be forgotten that the gift of doing good research is as personal as the gift of great painting, and once the men are found, the organization must be able to adapt itself to them, rather than expecting them to submit to restrictions which they find galling'.

Hill's memorandum served to keep the debate going within the Chamber, but there were no immediate results. However, in April 1959, Hill made the key move that was to mobilize a new industry research drive. Schonland, after a distinguished career in South Africa as director of the Bernard Price Institute for Geophysical Research and founder president of the CSIR, had become head of the British Atomic Energy Research Establishment at Harwell, and been knighted for his services. Hill proposed that Schonland, who was shortly to retire, be invited to conduct a review of the Chamber's research effort and its objectives. Because of Schonland's eminence in the scientific world Hill's proposal proved irresistible.

The Chamber accepted and Schonland agreed to carry out the investigation early in 1961. He duly spent three months in visits and discussions, and in studying the industry's needs, and tendered a detailed report. He pointed out that the chief objectives of the industry's research were the reduction of costs, the more effective use of valuable by-products, and the improvement of the health and efficiency of the labour force. These could best be achieved by the appointment of a director of research whose first function should be to draw up an expanded research programme. Schonland recommended among other departures, a more fundamental attack on the rockburst problem, vigorously directed, and on other important mining problems.

The report provided the foundation for a new approach to mining research. Mining houses had long pursued important projects on their own and would continue to do so, but the Chamber's role would greatly expand and, overall, research would be co-ordinated in the Chamber.

While playing his lively role in Chamber research as a member of the advisory committee concerned, Hill played a leading role in the fight against pneumoconiosis on another level. He was chairman for many years of the Pneumoconiosis Research Unit, a body administered by the CSIR and funded jointly by the Government and the Chamber, which pursued research in the fields of pathology, physiology and dust technology. Hill remained deeply involved too in measures to improve conditions for men working underground in Corner House mines. He was responsible for the modernization of the Rand Mines Laboratories and its location in new buildings on a 9-acre site at Richmond, Johannesburg. The group's metallurgists, chemists and physicists were provided with the most sophisticated equipment available, the envy of visiting scientists, and notable contributions were made to mine ventilation and dust suppression. Pneumoconiosis covers a group of lung diseases caused by breathing industrial dust; one of the most important being silicosis or 'miners' phthisis'. When silicosis first made its appearance on the

Rand at the turn of the century many miners contracted the disease after five years underground; by 1960 if a man contracted the disease it was likely to be after working for longer than 20 years in places where dust concentrations were high. The improvement was due to better ventilation, 'wetting down' of dust in stopes and development ends, and keeping workers out of dust caused by blasting.

Participating in a drive for better preventative measures in 1964, Hill declared at a meeting of the Mine Managers' Association that silicosis was still an occupational hazard, and called for further measures to improve dust standards. Men who rapidly contracted the disease were all too often those who exposed themselves to high dust and fume concentrations by disregarding the rules about re-entry too soon after blasting. People had to be shaken out of their lethargy, made more dust-conscious, and alive to the need for continually suppressing dust. The dangerous dust was invisible, most of the coarse dust being caught in the nose and throat. But silicosis need not be a hazard, for dust could be reduced below the danger level by good ventilation, and systematic sampling of the air to facilitate proper dust control. What was needed was a change of outlook, an awareness that in developing tunnels and in stopes microscopic particles of quartzitic dust constituted an invisible menace. Pointing the way that would result in pneumoconiosis being largely engineered out as a threat to the health of miners, Hill expressed as an equation the problem of making men change:

$$\text{Change} = \frac{\text{Driving Force}}{\text{Resistance}}$$

Change will come about if we have sufficient driving force, and if we concurrently minimize the other variable — resistance.

Hill was to influence advance in yet another direction by the encouragement he gave to Professor Herbert Sichel who pioneered the more precise valuation of the unmined gold in the ore bodies of mines on the Rand. The introduction of a sophisticated statistical method in sampling and assaying, and the interpretation of results, was to add a vital element to the operation of mines.

In the Sixties planning which was vital to the high-tech industry of the future proceeded against a grim background of political and economic turmoil. The decade was ushered in by an escalation of already endemic social unrest. Changes in National Party leadership had brought the idealogue and architect of apartheid, Dr H.F. Verwoerd, to the prime minister's office. His exceptional intellectual talents enabled him to give a spurious credibility to his fantasy of a country partitioned into separate states for Black and White. But an accompanying upsurge of racial unrest in 1960 culminated in the police opening fire on unruly protesters at Sharpeville, resulting in the death of 69. A shock wave of horror went around the world and universal condemnation of South Africa was intensified. Capital fled the country, and gold and foreign exchange reserves fell. South Africa faced the most serious balance of payments crisis since the events that preceded the departure from the Gold Standard in 1932.

Verwoerd's response was stern financial discipline, and a crack-down on political protest. A state of emergency was declared, and the Active Citizen Force mobilized. Thousands were arrested and detained without trial. The knock-on-the-door heralding the pre-dawn raid became a familiar happening in the lives of radical protesters.

Hill's position at the Corner House required that he personally keep a low political profile, though he supported opposition parties and joined the Progressive Party soon after its formation. Dora Hill had no inhibitions. She says: 'I was outraged by events, and determined to do something about it'. She joined the Black Sash, the women's movement, and with others who wore the sash of sorrow, stood in silent vigil in public places on important public occasions, to protest disregard of human rights and of the rule of law — and endured the indignity of being pelted by ruffians with overripe tomatoes and rotten eggs. She became Chairman of the Black Sash in Johannesburg, and a prominent protester. She says: 'I knew that this was potentially embarrassing for my husband because of his position at Corner House. But he was fully supportive of my right to protest and was not prepared to restrain me whatever the consequence to himself '.

Hill wrote to a nephew on 5 January, 1961.

Your Aunt Dora and I find life very full, she with her political activities and I with my professional work and such extraneous work as the University Council and the CSIR. Your aunt, as a matter of fact, has been so liberal in her views that we were really afraid that after the Sharpeville shootings she might be one of those who would be arrested. She used to go down often taking food parcels to the relatives of those who had been shot, and she has always been very forthright in declaiming against the racial politics of our government.

Hill had recently experienced a narrow escape of a different kind. On a family holiday in Greece he had been photographing classical ruins when he stepped backwards over the edge of an archaeological pit and plunged six feet downwards onto his head. He was knocked unconscious. To Dora he seemed to have mysteriously disappeared. She began a search and came on him trying to crawl out of the pit. Afterwards, Hill remembered nothing of the fall in which he was lucky not to have broken his neck. He was taken to a Greek hospital where his hands were held by young and glamorous Greek nurses. There his head was X-rayed, but unfortunately not his spine.

He returned to South Africa with his head swathed in bandages. Buster Fowler, who met the family at the airport, incurred the rage of Hill's daughter, Penny, by enquiring whether he had 'gout in the head'. In fact, Hill had injured his spine, impacting vertebrae which would eventually cause what nothing else would — his withdrawal from the golf course. But it would take more than 25 years to do it.

The choice for the key role of director of research at the Chamber of Mines fell on Dr W.S. 'Bill' Rapson, a vice president of the CSIR. He joined the Chamber in 1962 with the designation of Research Adviser. Rapson, a New Zealander, had obtained his doctorate at Oxford where he heard of a post becoming vacant in 1935 at the University of Cape Town. He went along to the library and studied available information about South African universities and academic work in his field of chemistry. Then he turned to the list of publications reporting progress in research and found — 'a bloody desert'. However, he took the post and enjoyed it and, apart from two war years on secondment to the Department of Commerce and Industries, he stayed on until 1945 when he came to Pretoria to join those pioneering the new-born CSIR.

Rapson's first task at the Chamber was to formulate a programme. In doing so he had to overcome resistance to any fundamental change in approach. It had been the custom to limit the Chamber's involvement in research to service functions, while research into underground mining techniques was left to the mining houses. Yet this was where the major part of mining costs were incurred.

Rapson saw that if the Chamber was to be involved in research on any scale, the vital focus of its effort had to be in the front line. But he found that mining house representatives on the advisory committees had not all grasped this, and it took a long time to get his programme accepted. Bill Rapson is a cheerful man who laughs easily, but he is determined, too, and becomes solemn and unyielding when asked to compromise on principle. He was simply not prepared to head the Chamber's research organization if it didn't do research into the technology of breaking out rock underground. His persistence won the day.

> It was a frustrating time because the Gold Producers Committee found it difficult to make up its mind. The modern generation of mining engineers was not yet on the scene; and there was an older generation who couldn't bring themselves to admit that research might solve problems which out of their accumulated experience and judgment they could not clear up out of hand ... I don't think the Chamber would ever have embarked on research as opposed to service at the time it did if it hadn't been for people like Pinkie. He had a very big part. He was a tower of strength.

On Rapson's recommendation the Chamber of Mines Research Organization (COMRO) was formally constituted in 1964. It included for the first time under the Chamber a Mining Research Laboratory as well as an Environmental Services Division, a Physical Sciences Laboratory, and a Biological Sciences Division. By then, the uranium-producing gold mines were contributing, via the Chamber, half the cost of the massive research programme launched in 1959 by the Atomic Energy Board into uranium extraction and processing to the nuclear fuel stage, and into the use of nuclear power in South Africa.

The research drive was given fresh impetus, too, by the Coalbrook disaster of 1960. At 7.30 p.m. on Thursday, 21 January, the workings of the colliery collapsed over a vast area. It was by far the biggest disaster in the country's mining history. It set in train the biggest rescue operation ever, but all was in vain. The 435 men at work perished and their bodies were not recovered.

The disaster was to bring many changes in the methods of extracting coal and in the planning of supports for workings. Up to then coal mining had relied essentially on accumulated experience. The inquiry into the disaster revealed that no scientific basis was available for the design of support pillars, and this led to the establishment, jointly by the coal industry and the Government, of the Coal Mining Research Council to direct research into safety in collieries. The Council's work led to the addition of a Collieries Research Laboratory to COMRO in 1966, and to the appointment of the outstanding Hungarian scientist, Dr Miklos Salamon, to head it. He would later succeed Rapson as head of COMRO and was to make a major contribution to hard rock mechanics, in both theory and practice.

Despite the initial hesitation, the industry's launch into expanded research in the 1960s reflected a bold spirit of optimism and enterprise during some of South Africa's darkest days. It was not at all an easy time to find funds for research. The gold price in United States dollars had remained at $35 a fine ounce since 1935, and the relief brought by the sterling devaluation of 1949 had been swallowed by inflation. In 1965, the Prime Minister's Economic Advisory Council, alarmed at the threatened decline in revenue and foreign exchange earnings from gold, called for an appraisal of the prospects for gold mining. A detailed study was made by the Chamber, submitted to the Council in November,

1966, and published under the title 'The Outlook for Gold'. It gave a gloomy picture of rapid decline, assuming, it was emphasized, no increase in the gold price. It warned that although gold production might continue to rise marginally for a few years more, the turning point was in sight, and once reached, the drop would be alarmingly steep. Output in 1966 was 960 000 kilograms at a realised value of R776 million, an output only achieved at the cost of a high rate of extraction of rich ores. In 20 years, the report forecast, the output might be no more than 160 000 kilograms valued at only R128 million.

In the event, production in 1986 would be 638 000 kilograms at a realised value of R17 billion, and the average price of gold would be, not \$35 as feared, but more than ten times that figure, while the higher price would permit the profitable mining of an average grade half as rich as that of 1966. In the 1960s nobody could foresee the soaring of the gold price that was to be a feature of the next decade. However, the Government decided to gamble on the gold price going up and introduced a comprehensive subsidy scheme to keep mines in being. By 1970 almost half the mines were running at a loss and enjoying, or seeking, State assistance.

Against this background the industry was called on to contemplate expenditure on research, knowing that the return on such expenditure would be in the medium or long term — or, as Plewman puts it.

> Or never! Or never! I used to tell mining students that research was like sponsoring someone to climb a mountain. There's the mountain. Here's the man. Give him equipment. Give him money. You organize a team of people to go with him. He may get there. He may not. You've spent your money. Nothing pays off unless he gets to the top of the mountain. And that's research. One

in 20 pays off, roughly. There are spin-offs though — ancillary things come out of it.

In a Rand Mines memorandum Hill wrote of research:

> This handmaiden of progress resists the view that problems cannot be solved. To her problems are a challenge ... To discourage research is to preach a gospel of surrender, and no executive of vision and spirit could accept such preachings ... Research is the tool whereby industry has solved and is solving its more intractable technological problems; it points the way and thus plays its part in co-ordinating action.

Rapson recalls that it wasn't at all easy to justify funds for research when the gold price was pegged at US $35 an ounce, and the outlook for the price was bleak.

> That was the atmosphere in which we were trying to get funds. The Gold Producers Committee was never difficult about proposals — the recommendations of the Research Advisory Committee as they came through were accepted. Nevertheless it was a terrible cloud hanging over one because you had to be responsible. And at that stage I still knew little of gold mining and had to rely on the judgement of others as well. You had to have an inner conviction carrying you through. Pinkie had that inner conviction. And I remember Jimmie Reid of Anglo Vaal was another. I used to love those two.

By the end of the Sixties COMRO already had produced an analogue computer for plotting the geometry of mine workings. An intensive investigation followed, reflected in a paper presented in 1969 on the application of digital computer methods to strata control. The paper, by Bob Plewman, Dave Ortlepp and Dr F.H. Deist, a Senior Research officer at COMRO, was awarded the Gold Medal of the South African Institute for Mining and Metallurgy.

The authors remarked:

> It may well be asked why the analogue or digital calculations of stress have any place in the field of mine design, since we have managed without such an aid for a very considerable time. The answer is, of course, a simple one. Where we previously had to guess, and frequently guessed very badly, a tool is now available to determine, in terms of the fundamental physical quantities of displacement, stress and energy release rate and what will happen at any point of the mine as a result of a particular piece of stoping. In short we can determine with a fair degree of accuracy, the change in field stress at any point in the mine, at any time in the past, present or future.

Such investigations were the forerunners of the massive digital computerization on which the mines rely today in designing mine workings that minimise the rockburst hazard, and facilitate cooling of the air. COMRO was already developing the rapid-yielding hydraulic prop which would yield rapidly to the irresistible thrust of rockbursts while continuing to provide support to the overhanging rock. Their installation provided a breakthrough of modern technology in deep stopes. Another early venture was the search, that still continues, to find a method of breaking out hard rock without the use of explosives and their attendant disadvantages.

With the advent of the higher gold price in the Seventies the industry was able to give its researchers more muscle.

COMRO was re-organized in 1974 and expanded rapidly, absorbing the buildings of the Rand Mines Laboratories in Carlow Road, Johannesburg. Important advances were made in the cooling of mines, in designing radio transmitters that would enable miners to talk through solid rock, in the application of hydraulic power, and in harnessing the potential energy in the head of service water in the mine. Research into rockbursts became sophisticated, drawing more on the science of seismology. Seismic networks were developed to monitor pressure phenomena in mines, and a search began for a reliable method of predicting rockbursts. There was a steady contribution to the advance of mining technology and to the improvement and safety of the underground environment. Annual expenditure by the mining industry through COMRO would increase from R2 million to more than R50 million in the 1980s.

In the Sixties Hill passed on the torch to COMRO's scientists, but his role in the launching of the new scientific basis to mining was recognised internationally. The Institution of Mining and Metallurgy in London in 1962 gave him its Gold Medal, its highest honour, in recognition of eminent services in underground research, and in particular to the problem of rockbursts.

President J.B. Simpson, in making the award in 1962 said that it was due to Hill's foresight and determination that research on the Rand had been organized on a wider and more scientific basis with the assured continuity of effort essential to success.

Hill responded by saying that when appointed to the ERPM 25 years previously he had had no inkling that it was to be the first link in a chain of chance leading to the Institute's gracious recognition of his part in ameliorating the problems of heat and pressure underground. He accepted the tribute on behalf of the mining engineers, scientists and administrators who had built up the research endeavour of South Africa's gold mines.

CHAPTER NINE

Some You Win ...

Throughout his years at the Corner House Hill gave high priority to new mining ventures. Rand Mines had inherited a chain of gold mines from its pioneer days, and had important coal interests, but mines, like men, have finite lives, and if the house was to maintain its position in the mining world new mines would have to be found to replace the old. On appointment to head office in 1947 Hill, made responsible for 'investigations', saw the need to move beyond the search for new gold mines and collieries. He explored far and wide for both precious and base minerals.

To find substantial deposits was one problem; thereafter the project had to pass the tests of its viability in the light of the likely market for its product; and the boards in Johannesburg and London had to be induced to allocate the resources, and to take the risk inherent in mining ventures. Propositions endorsed with enthusiasm by the consulting engineers did not necessarily win favour with those carrying responsibility for overall strategy and the 'bottom line'. So the hunt was not without its disappointments. Nevertheless it was pursued with undiminished zest.

In the early years Hill's attention was drawn to salt pans near Kimberley, and to the possibility not only of producing salt but soda ash, a chemical which had almost entirely to be imported to meet South Africa's needs, and which the Allies had found in short supply during the war.

Hill after exhaustive investigation in South Africa and America, believed that the proposition could have been pursued with profit, but it did not win favour, and it would be many years before a project of this kind would be developed in Southern Africa to match the expanding industrial needs of the region. Much effort was expended, too, in seeking diamonds in Namibia and Lesotho, and base minerals in the north-western Cape. The search went far and wide in South Africa, in Zimbabwe, Zambia and Mozambique, and at least yielded a clearer picture of potential, as well as a change of scene for Hill and his lieutenants, with some light relief.

One prospect visited was a copper mine in Zimbabwe among hills covered in deep bush. It had been found by a method used successfully by the old Rhodesian prospectors — by handing samples of mineral ores to the Matabele and saying 'go and hunt in the bush for rocks like this, and when you find it, come back and show me where'. It is recorded that Hill spent some time flying low in a light aircraft over the bush-clad hills in the bumpy air of high summer, to the violent distress of his companions — in a vain search for a site for a golf course. It was, however, decided not to acquire the property, later taken up by the Lonhro Group.

On another occasion Hill, Newman and Fowler went to inspect an iron ore proposition in the Transvaal, not far from Pretoria. They had been warned in advance not to reveal that the Corner House was interested as this would increase the price asked. It was decided to masquerade under false names, but the masquerade came hilariously apart when the trio became muddled over which names belonged to whom.

In 1960 exploration was given more muscle with the formation of the Rand Mines Exploration Company. Hill wrote to Engelhard on 23 March:

The whole job of exploration is at last being done systematically and well. All the skills needed are being drawn in — geological, legal, mining, metallurgical, marketing — and if we can't find mineral deposits or worthwhile ventures on which to embark, it will not be for want of trying.

While the search for some minerals came to a dead end, prospecting for platinum produced near-sensational results. In the central and eastern Transvaal the geological system known as the Bushveld Igneous Complex occurs. In this unique structure, geological chance has deposited most of the world's reserves of both platinum and chrome. Many options to mine platinum were acquired by the Corner House team in the Rustenburg, Lydenburg and Steelport areas, and platinum ores of unusually high grade were located. In 1966 a clear prospect of a platinum mine or mines emerged for the Corner House stable, the more especially so with Engelhard at the helm, for he was a man of enterprise, of quick decision, and of world knowledge of the complex platinum market. Engelhard however opted for membership of a consortium formed with Anglo American and General Mining and Finance Corporation (now Gencor) to deal jointly with the platinum interests of their groups, a scheme which seemed to offer advantages from the marketing point of view.

The consortium decided that the first platinum property to be exploited would be the deposit on the farm Brakspruit in the Rustenburg district, owned by the Corner House's Platinum Prospecting Company. It was further decided that the property should be worked on a royalty basis by neighbouring Rustenburg Platinum Mines of the JCI Group.

Rustenburg Platinum Mines in return agreed to sell to the

Platinum Prospecting Company the products of the ore mined in the tribute area for marketing through Engelhard Industries International. The arrangement saved the Corner House the capital cost of opening the mine as a separate producer, brought it earlier to production, with an assured flow of revenue, and absolved it from the risks involved in launching a new mine.

The fact that the arrangement looked at the time to have attractive economic and marketing features did not endear it to the consulting engineers at Corner House who had pinned great hopes for the group on itself operating platinum mines. They believed that the purpose of a mining house was to develop mines, and that it must be enterprising and accept associated risks if it wished to stay in the forefront of the mining business. They would ever after believe that a great opportunity had been lost. 'It was a bitter disappointment', said Newman. 'We could have cried'.

More than 20 years later Rand Mines would switch direction, taking a major entrepreneurial position in the operation of platinum mines and allotting to them the prime thrust of its investment muscle. It saw them as the catylyst which would propel the Rand Mines group into the 21st Century as a top mining house.

In the sixties however, all was to be overshadowed by the exploitation of the group's chrome ore interests. The chromite of the Bushveld Igneous Complex is a soft, easily-crumbled ore, occurring at shallow depth. However, it is so-called chemical grade, formerly of much less commercial value than the metallurgical grade found in Zimbabwe and elsewhere.

Metallurgical grade chrome was for a long time the essential constituent in the manufacture of ferrochrome alloys. These alloys are vital to the steel industry world-wide, particularly for the manufacture of stainless steel. The main industrial application of chrome is to prevent steel rusting. It puts the 'stainless' into stainless steel. Most stainless steel producers buy their chrome requirements in the form of ferrochrome which is produced by upgrading chrome ore through smelting.

From his earliest days in charge of exploration Hill urged the exploitation of the group's huge chrome deposits. The problem was that the prices obtainable for chemical grade chromite was little more than one-third of that paid for metallurgical. W.D. Galpin, a technical assistant to Hill, who had great experience of marketing metals in the United States, carried out a survey which showed that South African producers were being paid rock bottom prices for ore exported to Britain and America, much of which was then mixed with metallurgical grade chromite for the manufacture of ferrochrome. The prices obtainable for Transvaal chrome made its mining virtually uneconomic.

While Central Mining in London counselled patience in the poor market existing, Hill cast around for a solution, and found a possible answer in the ideas of his friend, Dr William 'Mickey' Bleloch, a consulting chemical and metallurgical engineer.

> I invited Mickey to lunch and took along Will Galpin. Bleloch told us: 'Your Company has chemical grade chrome, a material from which to date it has not been possible to manufacture ferrochrome. I think I can develop an economical process for sintering this and producing high-quality ferrochrome'.

Bleloch would add later: 'But it will take courage and megawatts to test it'.

Hill perceived that Bleloch's ideas were basically sound and won Gordon Richdale's support in 1951 for the setting up of a small smelting plant. There metallurgists succeeded in producing samples of ferrochrome from chemical chromite, using silicon as a reductant. However, the results were not conclusive, and further experiments on a much larger scale were recommended which required the erection of a full-scale pilot plant. Approval of the expenditure was not forthcoming and the project was shelved.

However the project was kept alive through a study of alternative processes set in train under Frank Bath, the Assistant Consulting Metallurgist. He was sometimes known as 'Chrome' Bath to distinguish him from his brother Walter, the General Manager of the Rand Refinery, who was known as 'Gold' Bath. There was also a 'Zinc' Bath and an 'Oil' Bath. Frank Bath's research showed that many of the alternative processes resulted in an alloy with a high-carbon content whereas the manufacture of stainless steel called for a low-carbon alloy. It was concluded that the Bleloch process which, all-importantly, promised the economical production of low-carbon ferrochrome, was the one to go for. Hill recalls:

> In 1959, we were able to persuade Engelhard to start a much larger research project. There would be inaugurated the first viable process for economically treating chemical grade ore for the production of ferrochrome.

Bleloch was given a five-year contract to act as a consultant to the Corner House in erecting a full-scale pilot plant at Crown mines and getting it into production. By the end of 1960 ferrochrome was being produced, though of somewhat unconventional composition. The new alloy was tested in the markets of Britain and the United States, and won approval. A plant at Driehoek, Germiston, was rented and a company called RMB Alloys (Rand Mines-

Bleloch) came into being. Frank Bath became General Manager. The Driehoek plant carried out feasibility studies and the metallurgists, setting aside all other metallurgical practice, grappled night and day with the task of turning a theory proven in a pilot plant into large-scale reality. On the basis of this, says Hill, the decision was made to erect a ferrochrome plant at Middelburg.

Since those days tens of millions have been spent on expanding operations — the start of the whole project being the genius of Bleloch; my specific role was to convince our directors that the way to utilize the group's huge reserves of chrome ore would be to embark on the making of ferrochrome and stainless steel.

On 10 August, 1962, Peter H. Anderson, Deputy Chairman and Managing Director of Rand Mines, wrote to Hill:

At a meeting of the Directors of Rand Mines Limited held today, it was decided to proceed with the erection of a plant for RMB Alloys (Proprietary) Limited at Middleburg, Transvaal, for the production of 10 000 tons of contained chromium per annum. In agreeing to the erection of the plant the Board acknowledged the important part you had played and the enterprise you showed in pursuing the idea of producing ferrochrome and other alloys, and it is my pleasure on behalf of the Board to pass these sentiments on to you. I know the decision means much to you and I can assure you that your concern for the future of the group is very much appreciated.

That 10 000 tons was to be the beginning of a huge industrial development. Bath now advocated that in addition to the production of ferrochrome, planning should start for the erection of another plant which would use part of RMB Alloys ferrochrome output for the manufacture of corrosion-resistant steel. There was complete confidence, he said, that the group was technically equipped to enter into the ferro-alloy and stainless steel world. Despite that confidence, there were problems and set-backs ahead. It would take not only courage and megawatts, as Bleloch predicted, but huge expenditure. However, from all this endeavour would come a major new export industry for South Africa, dominating the world supply of ferrochrome. The Middelburg plant was officially opened on 28 October, 1964. That year Rand Mines formed the Southern Cross Steel Company in association with the Eastern Stainless Steel Corporation of America.

South Africa's vast chrome reserves were thus released to swell the spectacular upsurge of its mineral industries. Over the 25 years after 1960 the value of asbestos production grew five-fold; of diamonds fourteen-fold; of manganese fifteen-fold; of copper eighteen-fold, and of chrome nineteen-fold. South Africa's minerals had become a vital component of the West's strategic reserves.

RMB Alloys, soon to be known as Middelburg Steel and Alloys, has since been joined as producers of ferrochrome by other companies, principally Samancor, controlled by Gencor, and Consolidated Metal Industries, controlled by JCI. By the end of the 1980s Middelburg Steel and Alloys alone would be reaching for a production of around 400 000 tons annually of ferrochrome. Overall, South African production would exceed one million tons, equivalent to about 40 per cent of total non-Communist world production.

Will Galpin, taking an overall look at the market in 1960, had reported: 'Stainless steel is at present enjoying the biggest boom ever ... but even so it is still only on the threshold of its potential development.'

He proved a sound prophet. Ferrochrome in South Africa, after a difficult and costly start, proved a tremendous winner. 'It was Pinkie Hill and Bleloch between them that did this,' says Newman, 'because previously the world wouldn't believe that Transvaal chrome ore could be used in ferrochrome production. Pinkie was the founder.'

By the mid-1950s Hill had acquired an international reputation. In 1959 the Government of the Indian province of Mysore (now Karnataka) sought through sources in London an engineer versed in deep-level mining to advise on the problem of heat and rockbursts on the mines of the Kolar gold-fields, then the deepest in the world. Hill was recommended and went to India in January and February of 1960. He found the Kolar mines hotter than their South African counterparts, with the rock at depth uncomfortably hot to the touch. He advised the concentration of mining operations and an increased rate of face advance. He stressed that concentration of the air available for ventilating the mine would accelerate air flow to the velocity necessary to lower the temperature of those labouring in hot places, both by direct cooling of the skin and by the evaporation of perspiration.

He attended a congress of the Mining and Metallurgical society there and gave an address on the experience of mining operations at ERPM. He also attended an address by an Indian general with surprising results. At a prior reception he found himself seated next to the general's daughter who later introduced Hill to her father. In the discussion which followed Hill mentioned his admiration for the Indian Prime Minister, Jawarharlal Nehru. The general responded by saying that during Hill's forthcoming visit to Delhi he should call on the Prime Minister.

Hill thought no more of the matter, but on arrival in Delhi received a telephone call inviting him to meet Nehru. He was warmly received. In the following discussion, Nehru spoke frankly on the issues confronting him. Hill was impressed by his approach to the threat to India then posed by the incursion of the army of Red China along thousands of miles of India's northern borders with the potential, soon to be realised, of armed clashes. The Indian people, Nehru said, were clamouring for him to meet immediately with Chou en Lai, the Chinese Premier, but he was determined to bide his time. He first wanted the facts to be established and preliminary discussions to be held at lower levels. The differences of view might thus be watered down, and by the time he met Chou en Lai, the dispute might have reached the stage of near-agreement. For the two leaders to be faced with an 'either-or' situation could well be disastrous, for neither would be prepared to retreat and lose face.

Nehru then told Hill about his plans for producing more food and industrializing India. He had dedicated himself to the stupendous task of raising India from the morass of poverty, and he wanted to do so by uniting the people in a common purpose. He was averse to coercion and violence, and wanted to bring about change by democratic means. He had no wish to emulate the methods of Russia and Red China.

Inevitably, the talk turned to South Africa's problems.

> Nehru told me that he believed in evolution and that the divine purpose was that all human beings should develop to their utmost, and that mankind should thus develop. People couldn't grow without responsibility and freedom. If clamps were put on people the purpose of the Divine was frustrated. He said that under apartheid we

were suppressing Blacks, and this was quite indefensible on moral and philosophical grounds. I could only agree.

Nehru enquired about Hill's plans of travel in India, and suggested other places he might visit. Thereafter, Hill's travel arrangements were made easy, and he was able to go wherever he wished despite the fact that South Africans were generally neither welcome nor accepted in India. With Nehru's help he was shown the industrial development that was being fostered, and given an insight into the work being done to raise the standard of living. He left India admiring the devotion of those grappling with the problem of poverty, but depressed by its immensity; an impression heightened by the contrast of a visit later in the year to the United States. He spent five weeks in New York 'surrounded by wealth surely unsurpassed in any part of the world'.

World travel became a regular part of Hill's schedule. There were congresses to attend in France, East Germany, Australia and New Zealand, and visits to the countries of the Far East. There were few countries in the world that he did not visit, and his experiences ranged from blissful to hair-raising.

In July, 1967, the Fifth International Mining Congress was held in Moscow. Hill was chosen by the mining industry to present a paper there, in association with J.B. 'Barry' Mudd, Consulting Engineer of the Anglo American Corporation, on 'Deep Level Mining Practice in South Africa'. A second paper on 'Deep Level Mining Research' was presented jointly by Gunter Denkhaus, Bill Rapson and Neville Cook. The usual problems arose for those visiting Russia, especially South Africans — the obtaining of a visa.

It was made clear at the outset that visas would be granted only to the five South Africans presenting papers. A letter duly arrived from A. Kuzmitch of the Congress office in Moscow, advising Hill that fees would be waived for him as the author of a paper to be presented. Thereafter: nothing. The visa did not materialise. It was established that the Russian Organizing Committee had asked the Soviet Foreign Office to issue visas, but by May no approval had been given. The delegates were told by those representing their interests in London that the usual Russian technique was to take no action if they did not intend to issue a visa.

On 3 July, a week before the opening of the Congress, Hill wrote to Kuzmitch saying that he was flying to Paris, and would go to the Russian Embassy to see if his visa had been granted. He followed the letter with a cable the same day: 'Paris office advised me visa refused because no vacancy congress. Cannot understand. Am going to Paris'.

His endeavours in Paris were not rewarded. No visa was forthcoming. Hill, nothing if not a man of quiet determination, flew to London. There he badgered, or charmed, the Russian Embassy into issuing the visa, only to find on arrival at Moscow that his name did not appear on the official accommodation list. In bureaucratic Russia this was a barrier to entry. Frustrated again, Hill sought the aid of a friendly travel agent who, by chance, knew that a man called Howard, whose name was on the list, was not coming. With the travel agent's assistance, Hill bluffed his way through the controls, entering Russia under Howard's name and took part in the Congress, though he carried with him a burden of trepidation about the consequence of discovery.

At the Congress he and Mudd were able to table their prepared text giving a picture of South African mining achievement. They were not able to expand much on it, because little time was accorded for presentation or discussion of any of the papers presented. The main gain from attending the congress was the opportunity provided for discussing common problems informally with mining personalities from other countries.

Nevertheless, the South Africans were able to place on record an account of advances achieved and to show a film on shaft sinking made by the Anglo American Corporation. Hill and Mudd's paper told of new developments in the siting of shaft systems, and in the arrangements for handling men, rock and material in them. No mining activity, they said, had presented such opportunities of technical advances in every aspect of mining engineering as gold mining in South Africa. This was particularly true in the development of a fast shaft-sinking practice which had led to the attainment of many shaft-sinking records. Current views were given on shaft dimensions, winding facilities, the passage of ventilating air through shafts and haulages to the working places, and the practical considerations involved in providing large-scale refrigeration for conditioning the air. They reported that problems with regard to rock mechanics had been approached on the widest possible front, and as a result of research during the previous 15 years there had been significant advances in knowledge and improvements in technique. The techniques found to be most successful, thus far, in lessening the number and severity of rockbursts were longwall mining — with special attention being paid to the sequence of mining and the shape of unmined areas — and the use of maximum support in the worked-out stoping areas.

This was illustrated by the experience at ERPM. In 1941 the stoping system on ERPM was such that large numbers of remnants were formed. With this so-called scattered stoping, the incidence of rockbursts was 1,2 for 10 000 tons mined, whereas in 1966, despite the greater depths of mining, the incidence with the new longwall method of stoping was only 0,6 per 10 000 tons mined.

South African deep-level stoping practice was based not only on experience but on the systematic study of more than 5 000 rockbursts in various deep-level mines. These showed convincingly that the planning of stope operations should have as a main aim the avoidance of remnants and face irregularities.

South African gold mines had then reached a maximum depth of about 3 350 metres. Hill and Mudd concluded by posing the question: What is the greatest depth likely to be achieved?

> From our current knowledge the answer would seem to depend primarily on economics, the greater the depth the greater the capital expenditure and the longer and more costly the lines of communication; the heat problem, too, aggravated by increasing depths, means that more money must be spent on air conditioning; containing the rockburst hazard to give reasonably safe mining conditions might entail our leaving a significant proportion of unmined ore which means loss of gold and also adds to mining costs. It would be, perhaps, not unrealistic to suggest that an economic depth of 4 500 metres will be attained.

It was not unrealistic. In 1972 Neil Armstrong, who not long before had brought to earth a piece of rock from the surface of the moon, visited Johannesburg and was presented with a suitably mounted and inscribed piece of rock taken from 3 394 metres below surface at Western Deep Levels Mine. In 1989 the Guiness Book of Records described the mine as 'the world's deepest at 3 582 metres, at which depth the ambient rock temperature, is recorded as 131 degrees F or 55 degrees C'. The mine's officials were proud of their achievement in providing an acceptably-cool working environment under these conditions. Shaft sinking and development were a continuing process with the prospect of a depth below 4 000 metres, moving towards 5 000 metres in the course of the 21st century. And as older areas decline fast enough to cast an economic shadow on South Africa's future, the 'ultra ultra' deeps beckon as new areas yield their secrets to the drills of the exploration teams.

Although Hill and Mudd, like the other 53 authors of papers at the Moscow Congress, were not given time to elaborate on their paper, they aroused enough interest to evoke an invitation from Soviet engineers to attend a special meeting on shaft-sinking techniques. The meeting was attended by ten Soviet engineers, and occupied a full morning. With the help of an interpreter an exchange of information took place with most of the 'give' on the South African side. Hill and Mudd were closely questioned on the use of cementation techniques perfected in South Africa to prevent flooding by sealing water fissures with injections of a cement slurry ahead of the sinking shaft.

The Congress was the fifth of the international series held in various countries since 1958 at which delegates were provided with the opportunity to visit mines and research facilities, and taken to show places of national pride throughout the host country. Similar tours were provided for delegates to the Moscow Congress, but Soviet Russia in the regime of Brezhnev and Kosygin was not an easy place to travel in. Despite the friendly endeavour of Hill's Congress hosts, he could not be fitted into any of the mining tours. The Intourist Agency was adamant in saying that his name was not on any list. Even those who were on the list did not find it easy.

Bill Rapson reported on his return to South Africa:

The complications and frustrations with which the traveller in Russia is faced have to be experienced to be fully appreciated. They leave him with little opportunity or energy to follow other pursuits in the first few days after his arrival. Since most participants from the West arranged their arrivals to coincide with the start of the Congress, their ability to participate was restricted accordingly.

Hill could do no more than visit the Exhibition of Mining Machinery which seemed to be well organized, and displayed a wide range of equipment, especially coal mining machinery, from 140 mining equipment companies. He did however attend the splendid performance of *Swan Lake* staged in the magnificent Palace of Congress by the Ballet Company of the Bolshoi State Theatre. It was 'a joy with a décor that was breathtaking'. However, as he did so with a ticket purchased on the black market, something which he had been warned was dangerous to do, his watchful unease increased, and he became particularly apprehensive about the cold scrutiny of an Intourist hostess.

He was happy to pass through the emigration controls at the airport, and shake off the fear of the heavy hand of officialdom on his shoulder.

Hill had been promoted from Chief Consulting Engineer to Manager, Techincal Services, at Rand Mines in 1964. Four years later he was made Group Technical Adviser, but the titles recognised rather than enhanced his position at Corner House.

Looking back on the years Dora remembers:

He always worked enormously hard. He never lost his temper, never got himself into open confrontation ... .

He was a perfectionist. Everything had to be just so, measurements not a fraction of a millimeter out. I am inclined to be impatient, want to get on with things. But he was quite right. When he made recommendations everything was thorough, set out in the minutest detail.

On April 2, 1969, in the historic Feather Market Hall in Port Elizabeth, Hill received the recognition of the scientific community with the award of the honorary degree of Doctor of Philosophy. The citation by the University of Port Elizabeth, after recalling his achievements in the mining industry, declared that as a member of the CSIR and of the Prime Minister's Scientific Advisory Council, Hill had made a notable contribution to the advancement of science in South Africa.

Retirement from Rand Mines came at the end of July 1969, at the age of 64. Hill had served Rand Mines in a period when the executive directors did not invite their technical manager (or chief consulting engineer) to join the Board. At the time, though, there was generally in the mining industry some reluctance to involve too much in top management the technical experts on whom the mining houses depended for the profitability of their operations and future expansion. The theory seems to have been that executive directors should consider thoroughly the advice of specialists but divorce them from personal participation in top-level decision making. That situation was in place at Rand Mines. It changed soon after Hill retired and vanished wholly after the merger with Thomas Barlow and Sons in 1971. It then became the practice at Corner House for the consulting engineer to be re-designated the managing director of the mines under his care, with a seat on the main Rand Mines Board. This pattern became general in the mining industry and served to remove possible communication blocks in the structure of top management.

Hill was undoubtedly frustrated at times during his career by his exclusion from important decisions. He could have sought high office elsewhere, but he remained loyal to the Corner House and warmly grateful for the rich tapestry of opportunity it wove for him. It may be that his absolution from ultimate responsibility freed him for an enhanced contribution to the wider mining industry and the community at large.

Looking back on his mining life on reaching retirement he declared it to have been a great and rewarding career. He enjoyed it all and, were that mythical choice opened to him, would choose it again. His advice to South African school-leavers, and especially for those entering university, was an unequivocal 'go mining, young man'. As ever the challenges, opportunities and rewards beckoned the enterprising.

In a long, warm letter of tribute to Hill on retirement, the Chairman, Peter Anderson, wrote:

> You may justifiably reflect with great pride and pleasure on a full and successful career which took you to the peak of the mining profession, and the Corner House Group is indeed indebted to you for the lustre which you have added to its name.

Ahead for Hill lay a fresh chapter of achievement. His contribution to the community was by no means at an end.

CHAPTER TEN

The Academic Streak

Throughout his working life Hill and his counterparts had to suffer the disabilities imposed on the mines by the Government's upholding of the colour bar and its championing of the White worker 'against racial competition'. By the 1960s in the face of the enormous strides in the economic expansion of South Africa, and the increasingly inadequate resources of white labour, that attitude had become Gilbertian.

In an interview with the *The Star* on his retirement in July 1969, Hill urged the government to allow wider employment of Blacks on the mines by easing the colour bar, which had been given statutory force as long ago as 1907, and maintained ever since despite opposition from mining companies. Hill declared that the four million Whites could not continue to supply the leadership and technical skills for a population of 20 million. He charged the South African Mine Workers Union (MWU), which represented White miners, with endangering the health of its members by opposing the training of Blacks to do routine portions of the work of ventilation, surveying and sampling officials. The work of those who collected samples of dust in mine air, in particular, played a direct role in the maintenance of healthy standards of ventilation in working places underground. A great number of these men were required, and not enough of them was forthcoming from the White population. There were far too many unskilled workers in relation to the middle group of technicians and skilled men. He urged that compulsory education should be extended to Blacks as part of the solution.

In 1964-65 the industry, treading delicately on the thin ice of racial prejudice, had attempted 'some moderation of traditional practices'. The Chamber of Mines had succeeded in negotiating with the MWU an agreement to a 'job experiment' on 12 selected mines. The Government Mining Engineer (GME) relaxed regulations to permit experienced Blacks to take over some routine duties from White miners. The selected Blacks proved what was generally known — that they were perfectly capable of doing more responsible work. The result of the experiment was higher productivity, and higher earnings and improved status for both Blacks and Whites.

To the Chamber's chagrin, its attempt to bend the colour bar unobtrusively was rudely interrupted by a break-away wing of the MWU which created enough rumpus to cause the Government to appoint a Commission of Inquiry. The Minister of Mines and Planning, J.F.W. Haak, then weakly backed off, stopping the experiment on the grounds that the Commission had found it to have 'disadvantageous implications'. The upholding of the colour bar on the mines, he declared, was to continue. The right-wing rebels, encouraged by their success, went on to capture control of the MWU. They then sought to block the advance of Blacks in ventilation, surveying and sampling, spheres of employment which fell under the aegis of the Underground Officials' Association of South Africa (UOA). The advancement of Blacks in these jobs had been done in consultation with the UOA and had nothing, per se, to do with the MWU at all.

The Government, nonetheless, was then still as ready as

ever to heed the protests of the MWU. The Minister of Labour, Marais Viljoen, (later State President), instructed the Industrial Tribunal to

> consider what measures should be taken to safeguard White persons employed on work connected with sampling, surveying and ventilation work on mines against inter-racial competition.

Hill was appointed as assessor to the Industrial Tribunal for the inquiry, together with P.J. Paulus, the fiery Secretary of the MWU, and another lively mining personality, P.J. Malan, General Secretary of the UOA. Together they visited 20 mines, from Messina and Phalaborwa to Welkom and Virginia. Not surprisingly, Hill and Paulus arrived at opposing conclusions. The MWU claimed that these classes of work affected the health of white workers, and the manner in which their contract earnings were measured. A position was being created, the Union darkly warned, in which friction could arise between Black and White, leading to the disturbance of industrial peace and raising the full possibility of a return to the unrest of 1964.

Hill found that in terms of practice and expressed policy there was no threat to the job security of Whites, and no need for 'job reservation', the latest euphemism for the colour bar. On the contrary, restrictive measures could be most harmful because the industry was faced with a shortage of White labour in these departments. There would follow an erosion of efficiency, the health of underground workers would suffer and hard-won benefits in the deployment of labour would evaporate. If a 'watch-dog' were needed for the interests of White officials, it existed in the UOA.

He reported:

It is indeed difficult to see why the MWU should concern itself so directly with the conditions of employment of groups of mining officials with whom they have no link. The Chamber of Mines and the UOA have reached an agreement that there will be no material changes affecting officials without prior consultation. This principle of consultation, of communication and discussion is of the utmost importance in bringing about change.

The Minister's answer was to bow to the MWU's wishes, and declare jobs in sampling, surveying and ventilation to be reserved for Whites — a decision carrying the implication that the employment of Blacks would only be permitted where exemption had been granted from the law. The MWU had demonstrated once again that the spirit of militant White trade unionism was alive and well. The absurdity of the situation would be underlined when no more than six years later the Government switched direction and conceded that job reservation based on race was no longer defensible or practical. The Government was not only willing to grant relaxation of the colour bar but to set in train its total dissolution. It declared that all races had an equal right to be trained and to qualify for any position.

Hill had found the time spent as an assessor to the Tribunal 'interesting and instructive', but disheartening because of the 'unbending, if not prejudiced attitude of one or two members'. Fortunately, there was a wide spectrum of other matters to engage his restless mind in his so-called retirement years. He was to be for the next decade the acknowledged expert on matters affecting the stability of ground, and in particular the erection of multi-storeyed buildings, and dwellings, on ground which had been undermined on or near the outcrop of the Main Reef running east and west along the Witwatersrand. He would be in constant demand, too, as an expert witness on mining matters in legal disputes. And he would play a leading role at the University of the Witwatersrand (Wits).

Early in 1970, Hill was asked to pass judgement on the stability of some building sites in the southern business section of Johannesburg which had been undermined in the early days. The owner wanted to erect a multi-storey building, but was unable to do so because of restrictions imposed by the Department of Mines. Hill saw that such restrictions were having a profound effect on the general availability of land for industrial building, and on the building of workers' homes near the city. His interest was fired and he began an extensive investigation to define the behaviour of ground on the surface above early mining operations. This was the beginning of a preoccupation that was to alter the skyline of Johannesburg and to increase the land available for the building of houses close to the workplace.

First steps were the examination of the records of the GME, followed by the sinking of boreholes and the establishment of a network of beacons. He became a consultant to the City Council on the use of undermined land. The GME proved ready to co-operate and to review the guidelines followed when shown to be justified.

Hill found on the basis of an extensive study of the behaviour of the surface across the previous 20 years that with the passage of time the shallowly-undermined ground gradually settled; pent-up stresses were released, leading ultimately to a state of stability and safety.

One of the most severe strictures on the building of houses was that none could be erected where the depth of undermining was less than 244 metres. This had prevented an extension of the township of Riverlea — where many hundreds of homes were urgently needed to cope with demand and the growing population. In December 1972 the

City Engineer asked Hill to examine the stability of the ground. The results showed that the whole of the area north and north-west of the existing Riverlea township was stable. Permission was granted for the building of houses where the depth of undermining exceeded 150 metres, a conservative concession in Hill's view, but one that was valuable economically and socially. He found great satisfaction that his survey cleared the way for these workmen to live close to their work, the alternative land being 35 km away. The new houses close to the workplace added to the quality of life of workers at Riverlea.

Decisions, Hill argued, must be based not on what happened in the 1903 to 1930 era when mining in the outcrop and upper sections of the mines was causing considerable subsidence. They should be based on the facts of the recent period from 1965 when virtually all mining had ceased.

In support of his argument he pointed to one important area running for some 25 km along the strike of the reef on which more than 320 beacons had been installed and monitored. The results showed that the rate of subsidence decreased with time until the ground reached a state of rest. With few exceptions, subsidence was *en bloc*, and not differential; it was slow and steady, and the rate was not directly related to the depth of undermining. The results of his studies were incorporated in a paper presented to the Institute of Mining and Metallurgy in 1981. Professor D.J. 'Sonnie' du Plessis, the great surgeon who became Vice-Chancellor and Principal of Wits, commented: 'It was a spendid paper which demonstrates the inquisitiveness that persisted throughout his life'. In it Hill declared:

> These facts should enable decisions on the use of undermined ground to be made with greater assurance than in the past. They should, indeed, have an overriding in-

fluence on such decisions, and the result would be more scope in the overall planning and development of the surface. The value to the country of a more flexible approach cannot be over-rated; the saving in direct and indirect costs could be tremendous...

Hill quoted in support of his conclusion the construction of Johannesburg's Western Bypass. Despite the fact that the Consolidated Main Reef mine had ceased mining in its upper reaches more than 40 years previously, the National Transport commission (NTC) was instructed to have the stopes under the freeway sandfilled to a depth of 244 metres to ensure its stability. When the cost exceeded R750 000 the NTC became alarmed and asked Hill to investigate. Hill, now approaching his seventies, spent a week crawling through the stopes left by early miners, and advised the NTC:

> You have wasted your money. The work done to date has been unnecessary. It's like filling a room with sand and saying the sand is supporting the roof. It is not. What is supporting the roof are the walls. In the area in question the compressed supports underground are supporting the surface and it is judged that subsidence would have ceased 20 years ago.

On his advice the NTC stopped the costly and ineffective sandfilling and bridged the actual outcrop with reinforced concrete.

Hill also drew attention to the expenditure of more than one million rand on the sandfilling of an area at the Modder B mine on the East Rand. The object was to safeguard housing, but it was questionable whether this expenditure was justified, especially as underground mining had ceased more than 30 years ago.

Hill ended his paper by urging that his investigation should be taken further by the appointment of a commission of inquiry. He was confident it would confirm that ground undermined at 50 metres depth was as stable as ground undermined at 250 metres. In February of 1984, Danie Steyn, Minister of Mineral and Energy Affairs, duly complied, and announced the appointment of a Commission whose work could lead to the release of large tracts of undermined ground. It became apparent that important social advantages in the regional planning of the 100 km strip of restricted ground between Randfontein and Springs would accrue from Hill's findings on stability.

Throughout his post-retirement years Hill was in demand as a consultant on projects such as the Verwoerd Dam and the Orange-Fish Tunnel, and as an expert witness in mining disputes. He found the degree in law taken at Oxford more than 40 years previously of great value in analysing cases of great technical complexity. The study of law, he says, is essentially an exercise in relevancy, and provides exercise in the application of the mind to the essence of the points at issue. It was also to prove an advantage when meeting head-on tough questioning by hostile counsel while on the witness stand. He positively relished such encounters, and was able to discomfort his opponents by his encyclopedic knowledge, and a gift for lightning riposte. Apart from his role in South African cases, he went to England to give evidence in a dispute on mining rights, and to Canada to participate in the successful defence of a defamation action brought against a newspaper for its exposure of exaggerated claims of the value of mineral rights held in South Africa.

But nothing was of more importance at this time than Hill's role in university affairs. Education had always been of vital interest to him. Back in 1944 he was elected to the

Council of Wits and he continued a member for 42 years. Inevitably, he involved himself in university research and encouraged links between university and mining industry researchers. He became chairman of the Bernard Price Institute of Geophysical Research (BPI).

Bernard Price, who had been General Manager of the Victoria Falls and Transvaal Power Company, had played a huge role in the advancement of electric power in South Africa. On his retirement in 1936 he founded and endowed the BPI. Basil Schonland became director. The original concept was that the BPI would address the problem of the interruption of power supply by lightning, a common occurrence at that time in the Transvaal. Price rightly saw that the Witwatersrand, prolific in storms of rare violence, was an ideal location to seek solutions to what was then a world problem. It was also an ideal location for the study of earth tremors occurring at shallow depths in the earth's crust, and the BPI contributed to the international search for a reliable method of predicting them. It has contributed importantly, as well, to the related phenomenon of rockbursts, and participated in the mining industry's expanding research into the problem and, in particular, in the development of the seismic network that monitors seismic events in mining. The BPI established a seismic network underground at ERPM in the Fifties, the first of its kind in the world. In today's new world of mining, industry seismologists along with engineers and scientists, monitor seismicity 24-hours a day. They are adding steadily to the store of knowledge leading to the ever-greater understanding of rockbursts that will perhaps make it possible to predict where and when they will occur.

Hill became Chairman, too, of the Board of Control of the Nuclear Physics Research Centre, later designated the Schonland Research Centre for Nuclear Sciences. In this role he renewed an association with the brilliant physicist, Professor J.P.F. 'Friedel' Sellschop, who was its director. Sellschop, while studying for his doctorate at Cambridge in the late fifties, enjoyed a close relationship with Schonland, then Director of the U.K. Atomic Energy Research Establishment at Harwell. Sellschop had received offers of employment from the United States but, urged by Schonland, applied for and was appointed to the post of Professor of Nuclear Physics at Wits at the age of 26, the first Chair in the field to be established at a South African university. Soon after, Hill gave Sellschop facilities at ERPM to hunt for the elusive members of the sub-nuclear family known as neutrinos. The search for them at ERPM was to prove internationally important in the study both of elementary particle physics and of the Universe.

Sellschop, now Deputy Vice-Chancellor (Research) at Wits, has vivid recall of a remarkable scientific achievement. In the Sixties he travelled to the United States, and lectured at the Case Institute of Technology. There the Professor of Physics, Fred Reines, brought him up to date on his quest for the neutrino which had culminated in his establishing its existence in man-made form. Reines and Sellschop, at dinner after Sellschop's seminar, agreed that it was now vital to prove the existence of the neutrino in nature, and argued that this could best be done very deep in the earth's crust, under conditions which minimized interference by unwanted cosmic radiation. Sellschop urged that the ideal location would be deep down in a Rand gold mine. Then back home in South Africa, he set out to win the support of one of the mining houses, but his first approaches met with a discouraging response, and some muttering about costs and profit loss.

My reception from Hill at Corner House was altogether

different — he was at once alight with the excitement of the chase. We went out to ERPM with Mischi Barcza, equally enraptured, for discussions with the General Manager, G.B. Hamilton. There it was agreed with the minimum of red tape, and the absence of talk about rands and cents, to create facilities at the deepest level of the mine actually ahead of stoping operations, so that the site prepared for us would conform to future mining needs and could be written off against its costs. I was able to go back to Reines with the offer of unique laboratory space at the bottom of the deepest mine in the world. This response was typical of Hill's natural affinity and effervescent enthusiasm for scientific research.

The neutrino project at first ran into difficulty and delay. The United States Congress was reluctant for work of this scientific prominence to be done in South Africa, for political reasons. However the only other possible site was in the Kolar gold-fields of India. Investigation showed this not to be comparable with the opportunities offered by ERPM. The interruption did not dampen Hill's ardour at all. With funds flowing from the United States, Sellschop was enabled to embark on highly significant research.

The neutrino, first postulated by Pauli in 1933, had been detected in the laboratory only in 1956. It reacts with matter only in what Sellschop calls 'a very wraithlike way', but carries energy, and has been found to play a pivotal role in the organization and order of fundamental particles. It travels at the speed of light, and as such arrives from outer space. It is one of few truly stable particles, it has zero electric charge, and — wait for it — 'zero rest mass within the current limits of experimental error'. No wonder perhaps that a journalist, observing Sellschop and his scientists and students absorbed in their esoteric hunt in the deepest laboratory in the world, should recall the lines from the *Pyschoed* by Hughes Mearns.

> As I was going down the stair
> I met a man who wasn't there.
> He wasn't there again today,
> I wish, I wish he'd go away.

The results of the research however were wholly positive. The neutrino, at the end of its cosmic journey, was trapped in the ERPM laboratory and for the first time was proven to exist in nature. The United States provided funds for a new laboratory, and the name ERPM won a prominent place in scientific literature.

Sellschop reflects:

> It was a momentous series of discoveries, one following the other in seemingly endless succession. It put this country in the forefront of research; it was good for the world of physics and astrophysics. The flow of discoveries was discussed world-wide. The ERPM work was the opening move in the long-awaited field of neutrino astronomy, because neutrinos are undeviated in their relentless passage through space.

He adds:

> It was a particular characteristic of Hill's that he had a deep insight, a gut feeling of what was truly meaningful and basic in research, and in particular for what was being courageously attempted by young researchers. As my Chairman he was a bulwark of strength to me, as he was in other University offices. He was no good at all in

raising money — he was too sensitive for that — but in all other ways he was immensely supportive. He did much to help academic researchers not to despair, and to maintain their confidence and sense of purpose. He was scornful of barriers to research progress, including those of finance!

As chairman of important committees he succeeded because he was blatantly genuine. With Hill there were no machinations. All who had to deal with him were confident that there was no hidden agenda.

Hill went on to become chairman of the Research Committee which had overall control of the research activity at Wits. The current Principal and Vice-Chancellor, Prof Bob Charlton, says:

> Research has always been a vital function of the university. If academic staff are not involved in probing the frontiers of knowledge in their field they are not really university people. Hill was interested at a very practical level in just what research people were doing, whether it was to do with analysing fossil dinosaurs from the Karoo, or nuclear physics research, or what the doctors were doing in the way of transplanting organs. He was fascinated by everything, and his input and enthusiasm, and the interest he showed was a positive factor in encouraging research workers to produce.

Dr Bill Rapson, who served under Hill on the Wits Research Committee, recalls:

> We'd sit down to a meeting with a long agenda at 2:15 and be finished by half-past four. This was because unless there was a point of principle involved he did not en-

courage detailed discussion of the recommendations of the responsible university staff. A point of principle was another matter. He never encouraged unnecessary changes to the proposals of the responsible university staff — that's the way to get things to run reasonably smoothly.

Hill was involved at Wits at another level, his belief in the importance of scientific management. As early as 1948 he was associated with Prof C.S. Richards, head of the Department of Economics, in advocacy of a Graduate School of Business Management and Administration at Wits. In 1968 he helped Richards to bring this dream to fruition. Richards became its first Director, and Hill joined its Advisory Board. It has achieved much in enhancing the efficiency of South African business.

Both at Wits and at the CSIR Hill was invaluable when there were differences to be ironed out between academic personalities, some of whom were liable to be contentious and over-concerned with the privileges of position, or lines of authority. Hill had the gift of achieving a compromise when none seemed in sight. He so disarmed people that contentions sometimes dissolved into thin air, so that people — and even Hill himself — came away from the meeting wondering what all the fuss had been about.

Of one such occasion, Rapson commented:

> He handled that very well. His slightly hesitant, tentative approach to things, you know, was just what was needed. Anybody who came in with the idea that the object of the inquiry was to assess blame would have been lost. He charmed everyone. It was a stroke of good fortune that somebody was available with the legal background and the personality.

In more general terms, Rapson commented:

> The thing that really distinguished Pinkie was his relations with other people. First of all his humanity, and coupled with this, his humility. He's a very, very able person and yet his typical approach in discussing a problem was that he knew little about it. He tended to put you in the position of authority speaking to him. The other thing that was important was his very strong sense of academic values, and a tremendous respect for scholarship and expertise wherever he encountered it. This was both a strength and a handicap. It was a strength in his relations with the CSIR, but at times a handicap in his relations within the mining industry, in that he did not only have an engineering approach to problems. His far-sighted approach could appear way out at times to those more preoccupied with immediate issues.

Hill's involvement in academic affairs attracted some criticism at Corner House in his early years at head office, as did his absorption in personnel management, work study and industry research. This was especially so when — which was nearly always — consulting engineers were swamped by the demands on them in solving the current problems of mining, of labour relations and of overall industry affairs. Hill defended vigorously his 'unswerving faith in the scientific approach', declared that his membership of the University Council and of the CSIR enhanced the value of his services to the Corner House.

> Contacts with members of these bodies are stimulating and tend to promote a breadth of view which I consider unattainable by the senior executive who immerses himself in the details of his immediate problems only;

and any organization or department that neglects the broad approach, connoting as it does long-term views and long-term planning, could justly be criticized as having inadequate leadership.

In my judgement it is of fundamental importance for the continued technical advancement of the Group that in these three fields — personnel work, study and research — standards must be improved.

He agreed that dedicated efforts were required towards the solution of the many urgent domestic problems, but emphasized

> I cannot agree that scientific method and the long-term view should be sacrificed. There are many willing hands to give help to the *ad hoc* problems. Someone or some group of people must see that the methods are right and that the future is not forgotten.

Hill's enthusiasm for university education and research has raised the question whether he would not have been more at home in an academic career. Professor Du Plessis comments:

> Personally I believe Pinkie would have made a great academic. He was a typical academician really. There was always the academician hiding behind the mining engineer.

Hill denies strenuously however that he was in any sense an *academic manqué* rather than a practical mining man. His heart was in the solution of the challenges that arise with everyday problems of deep-level mining. It was there that he found real fulfillment. Academic life could not have provided for him the satisfaction that came from the discernment of problems and the achievement in the relatively short-term, and under operational conditions, of a practical solution to them. He could certainly have entered academic life both early and late in his career if he had so wished. In 1955, Prof W.G. Sutton, Principal and Vice-Chancellor of Wits at that time, together with Prof G.R. Bozzoli and Prof L.T. Taverner, approached him with the suggestion that he become Professor of Mining. In accepting Hill's refusal, Sutton wrote:

> In making the suggestion to you Professors Taverner and Bozzoli and I were conscious of the fact that we had confronted you with a difficult decision because you already occupied an important position in the mining industry and were the sponsor and director of certain projects which were still to come to fruition under your guidance. We were confident that had you been able to accept the Chair of Mining Engineering you would bring to it a considerable measure of distinction and build up a Department which would enjoy international recognition.

Ten years later came a further invitation — that he allow his name to be put forward for the post of Principal of Natal University. Again he refused, saying that the thought of occupying so high and responsible a position was most appealing, but he considered that he had still a worthwhile contribution to make to the Rand Mines group.

After retirement from Rand Mines, Hill reached the culmination of his university involvement with his election to the Chairmanship of the University Council in 1972. The Council is the controlling body of the University in everything except academic matters which are the purview of the Senate. The appointment and dismissal of staff, the management of buildings and grounds are the Council's responsibility. Its annual budget is currently around R200 million.

The council is a disparate body of about 33. It comprises the Vice-Chancellor and his deputies and six members appointed by the State President, together with representatives of the City Council, headed by the Mayor, and of business and mining organizations, of the Council of Education of the Witwatersrand, of past students and donors, and of the Wits Convocation.

Professor Charlton comments:

> Chairman of the Council is a very important position in the University; a very close analogy is the chairman of a public company, as distinct from the managing director who is the vice-chancellor at a university. Certainly no vice-chancellor in his right mind would make an important financial or policy decision without letting the chairman know about it — without consulting him.

Hill is remembered as a quiet but strong chairman who kept proceedings under firm control without stifling expression of views, and who smoothed over differences of opinion in the disparate body so that, remarkably, it would come to face approximately in the same direction and adopt unanimous conclusions.

It was well that this was so because his appointment as chairman coincided with a new peak of student unrest. Persuading the council, as Hill did, to adopt an agreed statement on a student riot, was no mean feat. The troubles began at Turfloop, the University of the North, created by the quaintly-named 'Extension of University Education Act' which established separate universities for Black and Brown students in 1959, and barred them from the existing great centres of higher education. At Turfloop's Graduation

Ceremony of 1972 a student made a fiery speech of protest, and was dismissed. Then the entire student body, in uproar, was sent home. White students at the liberal universities of Cape Town, Wits and Natal came out in a vociferous demonstration of solidarity with their Black and Brown counterparts.

The demonstrations at the outset were focused on the racial inequalities existing in education. The focus soon shifted to the alleged brutality of police reaction, and the suppression of the right to protest. The dimensions of student unrest, and the violence of police response, were shockingly new, and crystalized in a police charge on demonstrators on the steps of St George's Cathedral in Cape Town.

The police over-reaction blazed images of brutal confrontation to the country and the world. There was uproar at Wits as the students, over-reacting in turn, made repeated attempts to march on the town. Police with troops of dogs, and led by high-ranking officers, swarmed onto the campus and 54 were arrested. The Times of London castigated the police for 'a remarkable combination of brutality, confusion and sacrilege'. According to the *Rand Daily Mail*, 540 students and sympathisers were arrested at the liberal universities in a week of student-police confrontation.

At Wits a mass meeting of staff and students was called, thought to be the biggest held there so far, and addressed by Professor Bozzoli, then Vice-Chancellor and Principal, and by Hill. Bozzoli declared that the universities were in crisis arising from the exclusion of Black and Brown from the established institutes of higher learning. The liberal universities had warned that the segregation of universities could not succeed, that the promise of equal (though separate) educational facilities was impossible to fulfil and that sooner or later the system would fail. It had now failed. There was something in the system that must be removed, and until it was removed, the tensions would never be relieved. Bozzoli said that he had sent an open letter to the Prime Minister calling for the strictly impartial investigation of grievances.

Hill, counselling the students to fight unjust laws within the framework of law, said that recent events had struck heavy truncheon blows at the cause for freedom. He declared:

> Many people would have it that students should devote themselves solely to studies and until such time as they graduate take small heed of the world about them. But how wrong can such people be? We live in a world of change — of uneasy change — and part of a university education should surely be to make students ponder on this problem, so that they can, both as students and later in life, contribute to solving the growing pains of our young nation...
>
> Laws should derive their sovereignty from a higher sovereignty — the sovereignty of justice, that final sense of rightness which has been implanted in the collective conscience of our civilization. It follows naturally that in the eyes of the law all men should be equal, irrespective of race, creed or colour.

Thereafter, a delegation called on Vorster, headed by the Chancellor, Dr. O.D. Schreiner, Bozzoli, Hill and Dr. W.B. Coetzer, the head of General Mining (now Gencor), who was a member of Council.

Vorster in typical fashion did not give the deputation much scope to argue its case. He said that he had no objection to student participation in politics, but he was opposed to street demonstrations which could so easily escallate into violence. Bozzoli recalls:

> He had a pile of cuttings from the Afrikaans Press on his desk, citing the rowdy behaviour of students, and we were never allowed to get around to what we had come for. We asked that the police should not come onto campus without asking the permission of university authorities. A useless request — they would continue to come whenever they wanted to with dogs, batons, helicopters, the lot. We got nowhere with Vorster.

Looking back on the events of that week in a Press interview, Hill said that he considered the students' protest about the inadequacies of Black education to have been a selfless one. Better education would allow a better utilization of labour and boost the whole South African economy. But the more serious aspect of the unrest had been the drastic suppression of the students' right to protest.

The trouble subsided. Student protest remained ever ready to surface thereafter, though the nature of the protest would shift. In half-a-dozen years the ban on Black and Brown students at White universities would lift, and they would soon form a large, politically-active and vociferous element at the liberal universities.

In 1978, Hill relinquished the chairmanship of Council, of which he remained a member, and became Chairman of the Wits Finance Committee. In December of that year Wits accorded him the honorary degree of Doctor of Laws.

Professor du Plessis, then Vice-Chancellor and Principal, told the graduation ceremony:

> He is not only an engineer and researcher, but a most humane person with a genuine concern for the advancement of man's welfare ... .

In 1972, his quiet demeanour, calm but decisive judgement and unquestioned integrity helped to ease the tension... .

... I have on many occasions had to rely on his judgement and support and this has been of incalculable value to me. A truly gentle man with ... an unfailing willingness to serve his community.

In honouring Francis Hill, the University is giving expression to the universally-held view that he is one of the leading contributors to the University, to our community, and to the mining industry, and in that to our country.

CHAPTER ELEVEN

Salt of the Earth

The passage of the years has not diminished the esteem in which Hill is held. In 1982 the South African Institute of Mining and Metallurgy gave him the Brigadier Stokes Memorial Award, created the year after Stokes' death in 1979 at the age of 96. It is awarded for the highest achievement and contribution by an individual South African in the field of mining and metallurgy, and is regarded as the most prestigious that can be accorded. The first recipient in 1980 was Harry F. Oppenheimer, the Chairman of Anglo American. The second in 1981 was Hill's old friend and associate, the brilliant chemical engineer and metallurgist, Dr William Bleloch who pioneered South Africa's electro-metallurgical industries. The third award went to Hill.

Mr George Y. Nisbet, the President of the Institute, said at the award ceremony that Hill's record of achievement in mining and metallurgy was 'immense and immeasurable'. His contribution to progress in mining, and the practical benefits gained in the mining and metallurgical field qualified him as an outstanding nominee.

In his reply, Hill paid tribute to Stokes as a man who combined the engineer's scientific approach with the spirit of the entrepreneur.

He concluded by saying that the award to himself:

Stems basically from the fact that I was fortunate in choosing a career that plunged me into an environment brimming with problems — opportunities to meet the unending and sometimes formidable problems that face a mining engineer in this country. Helping to combat them has been most exciting and most stimulating.

At that time Hill was withdrawing from public activities and finding peaceful occupation in the two acres of gardens at the Bell House with their view to the Magaliesburg. There were other pursuits and pleasures. He had long taken an interest in the Stock Exchange and given friendly advice to many. In retirement he had undertaken scientific study of the ore reserves of the various mines, and their degree of accessibility and development. Out of it came a fortune tidy enough to maintain a comfortable lifestyle. He enjoyed less-scientific gambling as well, including visits to the roulette tables at Sun City where he operated, naturally, on a scientifically-calculated system. Then there was golf, long kept up despite increasing disability originating in the spinal injury suffered in Greece long before. He is remembered for the length of his drives, remarkable for a man of his stature. He hit three 'holes-in-one' in his lifetime. T.L. 'Tommy' Gibbs, the former Government Mining Engineer, remembers playing with him on a course at Canberra noted for its 'dog legs'. Off the tees Hill consistently over-drove the fairways. He was a poor putter, though. At one time, true to his inquisitive spirit, he used a putter with an abnormally long shaft, and putted square on, and from between his legs.

Pinkie and Dora celebrated their Golden Wedding on 7 March, 1986, surrounded by family and friends. He could remember with amusement that when still a young man various insurance companies refused to insure his life on the grounds that he was a 'gouty subject'. To respond to a speech at the party he leapt on a chair with the spring of a much younger man, spoke as eloquently as ever without referring to a note.

The sons and daughters had long left home. David, the retarded elder son, lived at the Sunfield Home at Howick which Hill and others had founded. Margaret, the elder daughter, had gone to the University of Cape Town after a period in Paris learning French. Her young sister, Penny, had followed her to the Cape, joining the Cape Town Ballet School. A lovely and talented dancer, she was soon dancing principal roles and toured the country. Her parents were wholly supportive and in the audience, whenever possible. There is an almost plaintive note, though, in a letter from Hill, remarking on the difficulty of accommodating 40 dancers on a visit to Johannesburg. Penny was destined for the Royal Ballet in London when disaster struck in the shape of a torn ligament. To fulfill an engagement she danced on it too soon and permanent damage resulted, ending dreams of stardom. Penny would marry young, and settle in England.

Oliver, the second son, went to school at Bishops in the Cape. He showed great promise and was the star pupil in maths, but altogether failed to reach the standard in that subject in the entrance examination for a science degree at Cambridge. He took an honours degree in chemistry at Wits. From there he enrolled at Harvard Business School. Before leaving South Africa he married a friend of Penny's, a fellow dancer from the Ballet School. Then he worked for a while with Engelhard Industries in the United States before taking his Master's degree in Business Administration. He returned to South Africa, and invited an American fellow student at Harvard, Charles Parsons, to spend a fortnight's holiday at the Bell House. Margaret had completed her degree at Cape Town, followed by post-graduate study in librarianship, and was working out of London as an air hostess with British European Airways. She chose that moment to come home for a visit. She and Parsons fell in love and were soon married. Their home is near New York, but Margaret is a frequent visitor to her parents in Johannesburg.

Oliver vowed that he would never work in a chemical laboratory. Instead he set his sights on the dizziest heights of the business world, and promised his father a Rolls Royce when he reached that goal. He displayed entrepreneurial brilliance and honoured his promise.

In 1976 Oliver achieved public notice with his declaration that dynamite as a mining explosive was dead. He obtained the licence for Tovex, the water-gel explosive widely used in the United States, and set out to obtain a major share of the mining industry's business. Tovex has certain advantages, particularly in its high safety factor, but the mining industry was not going to switch without extensive testing, and tended to stay with their long-standing dynamite contracts with African Explosives. Oliver Hill, however, was soon expanding into fertilisers. Then demand plunged as drought plagued major farming regions. The fertiliser company went into liquidation, and Oliver became insolvent. He was soon involved in new ventures, leaving South Africa in December 1987. Then, in 1989, the South African Police announced that a warrant was being issued for his arrest in connection with foreign exchange irregularities, amounting to R170 million. In a statement from London published in the *Sunday Times* on 28 May, 1989, Oliver Hill admitted to having been involved in certain transactions, though of a substantially lower order than those alleged. But he declared that they had only been conducted on the advice of eminent counsel that they were legal. There, at the time of writing, the matter rests. Dora and Pinkie Hill were left 'holding thumbs hard' that all would come out well for their son.

Meanwhile, in 1988 at the age of 82, Hill had received the accolade of the wider engineering profession. At a ceremony in January of that year the Federation of Societies of Professional Engineers (FSPE) gave him the FSPE award for services to the profession. In making the award, Professor A.N. Brown, the President, said that Hill had been singled out for the award as an engineer, mainly, but also as a scientist, researcher, innovator, manager, and leader of men.

> But neither his achievement as an engineer nor his passion for scientific research obscure his humaneness and concern for the advancement of man's welfare. Concern for his fellow men lay at the heart of his research efforts relating to the problem of rockbursts, problems of heat and humidity and of the dust that results in pneumoconiosis. Another problem was the traditional dictatorial and conservative management style within the mining industry. The introduction of the principles of scientific personnel management has greatly improved the lot of persons engaged in the industry ... In dealing with men, his behaviour has always been characterized by dignity, tact, charm and courtesy.

The following year Hill was bidden to Tuinhuis in Cape Town to receive from the State President the Order for Meritorious Service (Gold). The citation declared that Hill 'ranked with the most distinguished mining engineers ever engaged in the South African mining industry'.

Thus was summed up Hill's contribution at the end of his working life. He is a warm-hearted, kindly man, of incorrigible curiosity, and irrepressible spirit, who became the doyen of those who contained the primordial forces encountered as man thrust deeper into the earth's crust. He was the doyen too of those who evolved a matching approach to the human factors in mining. A generation of mining engineers followed the standards he set. And he sparked a research drive that has won recognition, and admiration, throughout the mining world. In the new South Africa now being evolved, with all its promise and fears, the economic muscle of social progress will be nourished by the winning of wealth from the earth, down to the 'ultra ultra deeps', on the science base of mining technology bequeathed by Hill and men like him. Of such Kipling wrote:

> For their work continueth
> And their work continueth
> Broad and deep continueth
> Greater than their knowing.

What they did lives. So do the memories of shared laughter and good companionship in tough times and places.

Johannesburg, June 1990.

Index

Active Citizen Force 111
Administrative Staff College, Henley-on-Thames 94
Advisory Council for Scientific Policy 103
African and European Investment Corporation 66, 68
Altenburg, Saxony, tin works 40
Anderson, Peter H 127, 138
Angelo Mine 35
Angelo Reef 35
Anglo American Corporation 29, 30, 66, 68, 69, 123, 133
Anglo Vaal 80, 81
Applied Physiology Laboratory 107
aptitude testing at mines 88–9
Armstrong, Neil 134
Association of Mine Managers 40, 42, 47, 57, 110
Atomic Energy Board 104, 114

Bailey, Sir Abe 29, 67
Baillieu, Sir Clive (later Lord Baillieu) 70, 76, 83, 98
Barcza, Mischi 63, 149
Barlow, C S 97
Barlow Rand 55
Barlow, Thomas & Sons 137
Basal Reef 32, 67, 69, 76
Bath, Frank 126, 127, 128
Bell House 162

Benson, Robert *Firm* 97
Bernard Price Institute of Geophysical Research 147
Biesheuvel, Dr. Simon 87, 88, 90
Biological and Chemical Research Laboratory 107
Black, Alistair 91, 92
Blakeway, R E M 80
Bleloch, Dr William 'Mickey' 125, 126, 127, 129, 161
Blyvooruitzicht Mine 30
Boer, Frits 87
Bozzoli, Professor G R 155, 157, 158, 159
Brakspruit Farm, Rustenburg 123
Bridges, Dr Rodney 73
Brigadier Stokes Memorial Award 161
Britannia Mine 63
Brown, Prof A N 165
Bryant, Roy 78, 79
Bushveld Igneous Complex 123, 124

Cason Mine 35
Central Mining 29, 30, 67, 68, 70, 83, 96, 97, 98
Chamber of Mines 56, 106–109, 113–116
Chamber of Mines Research Organization 114, 117–119
Charlton, Prof R 151, 156

167

Chemical, Metallurgical and Mining Society 44, 58, 102
Cinderella Mine 35
chrome *see also* ferrochrome 124
Coal Mining Research Council 115
Coalbrook disaster 115
Cochrane, D A 79
Coetzee, Dr W B 158
Collieries Research Laboratory 115
colour bar on the mines, attempts at relaxation of 139–142
COMRO *see* Chamber of Mines Research Organization
Consolidated Main Reef Mine 145
Consolidated Metal Industries 128
Cook, Dr Neville 131
Cooke, Dr J F K 80
Co-ordination Committee of mine managers 94
Copper Queen Mine 14, 15
Corner House 35, 36, 66, 67, 69, 70, 73, 74, 78, 80, 81, 83, 89, 95, 98, 103, 107, 123, 124, 137, 138, 153
Council for Scientific and Industrial Research (CSIR) 87, 103, 104, 106, 108, 152, 153
Crouch, H T 6

de Rothschild, Baron Elie 97
'Deep Level Mining Practice in South Africa' *Congress Paper* 131
Deist, Dr F H 118
Denkhaus, Dr H 'Gunter' 104, 105, 106, 131
diamonds, Namibia & Lesotho 122
Doornfontein Mine 35

Du Plessis, Prof D J 154, 159
Durban Deep Mine 49, 52–55, 62–65
Dust and Ventilation Laboratory 107
'Dynamic Administration', Presidential Address to Institute of Personnel Management 61

East Rand Proprietary Mines 32–38, 39–51, 99–100, 129, 133, 147–150
Eastern Stainless Steel Company of America 128
Engelhard, Charles 76, 77, 96–99, 122, 123
Engelhard Industries International 124
Erfdeel Farm 73
Erleigh, Norbert 71–74
Exhibition of Mining Machinery, Moscow 136
'Experience in support at depth at the East Rand Proprietary Mines, Ltd.' *Technical Paper* 42
Extension of University Education Act 156

Far West Rand 29, 31
Farrar, Sir George 35
Federation of Societies of Professional Engineers 165
ferrochrome, research into production 124–129
Fife Coal Company 15–18
Fifth International Mining Congress, Moscow 131–136
fire control 49–50
Follett, Mary Parker 61
Ford, J S 57
Fowler, A R C 'Buster' 22, 26, 74, 76, 82, 93–94, 113, 122

Freddies North Mine 70
Freddies South Mine 70
Free State Geduld Mine 70
Friedsheim 70

Galpin, W D 125, 128
Gardner, Robert 96
Geduld, Hole 1 69, 70
General Mining & Finance
  Corporation 123
General Strike, 1926 16
Gibbs, T L 162
Glaser Brothers 96
Gold Fields 29, 30, 68, 69, 72
gold mining subsidy scheme 116
Gold Producers' Committee 107,
  114, 117
Gold Standard 28, 36, 111
golf 162
Gorges, Ralph 92
Graduate School of Business
  Management & Administration
  University of the
  Witwatersrand 152
Great Depression, 1929 16

Haak, J F W 140
Hagart, R B 97
Hall, Noel 94
Harmonie (farm) 71–72
Harmony Gold Mine 72–82
Hart, Herbert 13
Hill, David sen. 8, 12
Hill, David jun. 85, 163
Hill, Denston 8
Hill, Dora (née Kotzé) 8, 23, 24,
  37, 64, 85, 86, 87, 112, 136, 162
Hill, Francis George, sen. 4, 5,
  8–9
Hill, Francis George 'Pinkie' (in
  chronological order of the text)
  At New College, Oxford 1–3
  University of the
    Witwatersrand 2, 7, 8, 20
  friendship with J H Hofmeyr
    2–3
  early life & education 4–7
  University Air Squadron 9–13
  International Conference,
    Budapest 13
  industrial psychology study
    13–14
  tour of USA 14–15
  career at Fife Coal Company
    15–18
  New Modder Mine 21–25
  marriage to Dora Kotzé 24–25
  Rand Mines 27, 31, 32
  ERPM 32–38
  rockburst investigation 41–42,
    47–49
  ventilation research 49, 52–55
  Durban Deep Mine 62–65
  President, Chemical,
    Metallurgical & Mining
    Society of SA 58
  President, Institute of
    Personnel Management (SA)
    61–2
  Consulting Engineer, Rand
    Mines 65, 71
  Harmony Mine 72–79, 82
  Head Office, Johannesburg
    83–87, 90–95
  Technical Manager, Rand
    Mines 99
  CSIR governing council 103
  mining research 106–108, 117,
    119
  pneumoconiosis research 109
  political inclinations 111–112
  accident in Greece 112–113
  Institute of Mining &
    Metallurgy award 119–120
  new mining ventures 121–122
  chrome research 125–129

169

overseas experiences 129–136
promotions 136
Doctor of Philosophy, UPE 137
retirement 137
undermined ground research 143–144
university research 146–154
Wits University Council 155–159
Hon Degree, Wits 159–160
Hill, Katherine Johanna (née Hauptfleisch) 4
Hill, Katherine (Renie) 7, 8
Hill, Penny 85, 113, 163
Hill, Robert Oliver 85, 163–164
Hill, Samuel George 4
Hill, Sonnie 6–7
Hill, Winnie 7–8
Hofmeyr, J H 2–4, 6, 9
Hofmeyr, Reinald 52–55, 87
hydraulic prop 118

ice-packs, experiments in underground mining 46–47
Industrial Tribunal Inquiry into job security on mines 141
Institute of Personnel Management (South Africa) 56, 61, 62
Institution of Mining & Metallurgy, London 119, 144
International Nickel Company 97
Iron ore exploration, Transvaal 122
Irvine, L G 44

Johannesburg Consolidated Investment Company 68, 70
Jones, Guy Carleton 29

Kingswood College 5–7
Knox, Lady 12

Kolar gold-fields, India 43, 129, 149
Kotzé, Sir Robert 8, 24–26, 85, 86
Krahmann, Dr Rudolph 29–30
Krynauw, A H 37–8
Kuzmitch, A 132, 134

Lawrence, W H A 71
'Letters from Home' 9, 12
Lewis, C S 1,2
longwall stoping (mining) 41, 43, 47–49
Lonsdale & Company 97

'Major changeover in the ventilation of a deep-level mine'. *Technical paper* 44
Malan, P J 141
'Management in Industry'. *Presidential address* 58–60
Martin, John 29, 67, 68, 71
Meiring, Piet 73
Mellor, Dr E T 29
Merriespruit Mine 80–81
Meyer, E C J 18, 21, 22, 37
Middelburg Steel and Alloys 128
migrant labourers on mines 87–89
Milne, Joseph 71, 73, 74
mine design, computer methods of calculation 117–118
Mines Engineering Brigade 34–35
Mineworkers' Union, strike 64
Modder B Mine, sandfilling 145
Mudd, J B 131, 132, 134, 135

National Institute for Personnel Research 87–90
National Mechanical Engineering Research Institute 104
National Transport Commission 145

Nehru, Jawarharlal 129–131
neutrinos, research into 148–150
New Blue Sky Mine 35
New Comet Mine 35
New Modder Mine 18, 21–23, 37, 53
Newman, Syd 75, 78, 80, 92–94, 122, 124, 129
Nisbet, George Y 161
Nuclear Physics Research Centre 147

Odendaalsrus 68–70
Ophirton Earth Tremors Committee 40
Oppenheimer, H F 97, 161
Oppenheimer, Sir Ernest 68, 69
Orange-Fish Tunnel 146
Orange Free State, gold mining in 31, 32, 66, 68
Orange Free State Investment Trust 69
Order for Meritorious Service (Gold) 165
Orenstein, A J 44
Ortlepp, David 90, 91, 118
'Outlook for Gold'. *Report* 116

paper-making industry 96
Parsons, Charles 163, 164
Paulus, P J 141
personnel management, Durban Deep Mine 53–61
Corner House 89–90
Petersen, Tony 94
Pickerill, V J 54
Pilgrim's Rest mines 95
Pim, Joane 75
platinum 123
Platinum Prospecting Company 123–124
Plewman, W P 63, 75, 78, 80, 92 94, 116, 118
Pneumoconiosis Research Unit 109
Precious and Base Metals Act, 1908 24–25
pressure bursts (mining) 47, 48, 51
Price, Bernard 147
Prime Minister's Economic Advisory Council 103, 115

Rand American Investments 97
Rand Mines 18, 27–30, 53, 55, 65, 67, 83, 98, 99, 104, 124, 128, 137
Exploration Company 122
Laboratories 109, 119
Rand Rebellion, 1922 16
Ranson, E C 44
Rapson, Dr W S 113–114, 117, 131, 135, 151–152
Reid, Jimmy 117
Reines, Fred 148
Richards, Prof C S 152
Richdale, Gordon V 71–74, 76, 82, 96, 97
Riverlea 143–144
RMB Alloys, Driehoek, Germiston 126–127
RMB Alloys, Middelburg, Tvl 127–128
Robinson Deep Mine 19–20
rockbursts *see also* pressure bursts 37–42, 47, 48, 91, 102–105, 118, 119, 147
Rockburst and Strata Movement Committee 106
rock pressure, research into 102–105
Roux, Dr A J A 104, 105
Royal Johannesburg golf course 77
Russell, Sir John 108

171

Russia, visit to 131–136
Rustenburg Platinum Mines 123

St. George's Cathedral, Cape Town protest incident 157
Saint Helena Mine 68, 69
Salamon, Dr Miklos 115
salt pans, Kimberley region 121–122
Samancor 128
Schonland, Dr, B J 108–109, 147–148
Schreiner, Dr O D 158
seismicity, monitoring of 159
Sellschop, Professor J P F 148–150
shaft-sinking, Durban Deep Mine 62
Sharpeville 111
Sibley, Brian 2
Sichel, Professor Herbert 111
silicosis 109–110
Simpson, J B 119
Smuts, J C 26, 27, 103
Smuts, Japie 26
soda ash 121
South African Forest Investments 96
South African Institute of Mining & Metallurgy 58, 106, 118, 161
South African Mine Workers' Union 139–142
South African Townships 67, 68
Southern Cross Steel Company 128
steel, corrosion-resistant 128
Steele, Ken E 37, 38, 51
Steyn, Danie 146
Stokes, R S G 28, 30, 31, 71, 72, 161
Stratten, T P 87, 90, 97
student protests, 1972 157–159

support systems (mining) 41
Sutton, Prof W G 155
'System of longwall stoping in a deep-level mine, ...' *Technical Paper* 47–49

Taverner, Prof L T 155
temperature control (mining) 44–46
'The Terraces' (house) 5, 8
Thiel, Edwin W 21, 81, 94
torsion balance 67
tree-planting on mines 64, 95–96
Trinidad Leaseholds 96

undermined ground, research into stability of 143–146
Unger, F A 30
Union Corporation 66, 67, 69, 87, 97
Union Free State Coal and Gold Mines 71
Union Observatory seismic station 40
University of Natal 155
University of Port Elizabeth 137
University of the North, Turfloop 156
University of the Witwatersrand Council 147, 155–156
  Finance Committee 151
  Research Committee 151
  student protest 157–158
uranium mining 80
Urwick, Col L 61

Valley Road (house) 86, 87
Venterspost 29
ventilation (mining) 37, 38, 43–47
Verwoerd Dam 146
Verwoerd, Dr H F 111
Viljoen, Marais 141

Virginia Mine 81–82
Vorster, B J 158–159

Walton, A J 27, 28, 31
West Driefontein Mine 30
West Witwatersrand Areas Ltd 29
Western Bypass, Johannesburg 145
Western Deep Levels Mine 134
Western Holdings 32, 66–69

wet bulb temperature measurement 44
Whillier, Dr Austin 44
'White Gables' (house) 85
White, Isabel 53, 61
Woodman, Herbert 14
World War 2, gold mining activity 34
Wyndham, Professor Cyril 107

Zimbabwe copper mine 122